John Eliot

An Apology for Socrates and negotium posterorum

Vol. II

John Eliot

An Apology for Socrates and negotium posterorum
Vol. II

ISBN/EAN: 9783337157524

Printed in Europe, USA, Canada, Australia, Japan

Cover: Foto ©Thomas Meinert / pixelio.de

More available books at **www.hansebooks.com**

AN
APOLOGY FOR SOCRATES
AND
NEGOTIUM POSTERORUM:
BY SIR JOHN ELIOT.

(1590—1632.)

NOW FOR THE FIRST TIME PRINTED: FROM THE
AUTHOR'S MSS. AT PORT ELIOT.

Edited, with Introduction and Additions from other MSS. at Port Eliot, Notes and Illustrations, &c.
BY THE
REV. ALEXANDER B. GROSART, LL.D., F.S.A.,
ST. GEORGE'S, BLACKBURN, LANCASHIRE.

IN TWO VOLUMES.
VOL. II.

NEGOTIUM POSTERORUM, PART II.—ADDITIONS FROM PORT ELIOT MSS.—
NOTES AND ILLUSTRATIONS AND GENERAL INDEX.

PRINTED FOR EARL ST. GERMANS AND
PRIVATE CIRCULATION ONLY.
1881.

CHISWICK PRESS:—C. WHITTINGHAM AND CO.,
TOOKS COURT, CHANCERY LANE.

NEGOTIUM POSTERORUM.

TOMUS SECUNDUS, LIBER SECUNDUS.

NEGOTIUM POSTERORUM.

BOUT the time of the adiornment of the Parliament from London, the Turks were growen verie infestuous to the marchants. divers ships & vessels they had taken, wth a multitude of captives, drawn from them. in the west parts they had made the coasts soe dangerous through their spoiles, as few dar'd putt forth of their harbors; hardlie in them was the securitie thought enough. the boldness & insolenc of these piratts was beyond all comparifon, noe former times having beene exampled wth the like. their adventure formerlie on those seas was rare, almost vnheard of, wch made their comming then more strange. that being aggravated by their frequencie & number, wch their dailie spoiles did witness, & those much heightend by their bouldness, it made a great impression on the Countrie, & possesst it wth much fear, that divers alarums it receavd, wch made divers motions in the people, who, as their manner is, fain'd or enlargd the cause after the apprehension of their fancies, wch passing to their neighbours, still affected them wth more, vntill it had a generall influenc throughout/ all

even the cheife townes & strengths not priviledgd or exempted. they had in some parts entred even into the mouthes of the close harbors, & shewd themſelves in them, & all the open roads they vs'd confidentlie as their owne. some ships they had taken vnder the fforts & caſtells. nothing did deterr them, but the whole Sea seem'd theirs. in Cornwall they had landed, & carried divers prisoners from the shore. all fishermen that stird became their prey & purchase. they had gaind in that Summer, at least, twelve hundred chriſtians, the loss of whom causd great lamentation wth their frinds. this man bewayld his sonns, that his ffather, another his brother, a foorth his servant, & the like; husbands & wives, wth all relations els of nature & civilitie did complaine; besides the preiudice of the marchants, the losing of their ships, the interruption of their trade, wch made a generall dampe on all things, commodities being not vendible wher the transportation is denied; this likewise made a generall crie & exclamation that noe part of that countrie did stand free, noe person but was affected wth that sence/ heerof a dailie intelligenc had been given to the miniſters of the State, wth speciall addresses thervpon to implore for some releife. divers ships were then readie of the ffleet, wch might have beene commanded to that service. they lay idle in their harbours, in the Thames, at Portsmouth, & elswher, all their men and provisions being aboard. they were to attend the preparation of their fellows, for wch generallie was appointed the Rendezvous at Plimouth; soe as this imploiment would have drawne them to that place. their countenanc in the passage would have dispeld those pirats. noe charge had beene occasiond to the K[ing] noe wast of the provisions, noe vnreadiness in the ships, noe disorder to the service, but rather an advantage given in all; yet nothing could be gotten, noe ship might be remov'd, the trade & marchants were neglected, the coaſt was left vngarded, the Countrie stood expos'd, as if in expiation of some sinne, it had beene made a sacrifice to those monsters. amongst other cries & intelligences of that kinde, ther came one directed to a gentleman of those parts, to whom it had relation by his office, being vice admirall/ of devonshire, that ther were fowrtie saile of Turks beſides those w[ch] formerlie kept that coast, then in one ffleet come w[th]in the channell, & this warranted by the deposition of the maſter & some others of a small barke that had past them in the night. he represents it to the K[ing]. the K[ing] resenting trulie the danger of his subiects presently recommends it to his Councell, commanding that gentleman to attend them; who meeting, & having the conſiderations laid before them of the diſhonor to the K[ing], the preiudice to the Countrie, the necessitie & facilitie of releife, for w[ch] some few good ships would serve, & those, being readie, importing noe charge vnto the K[ing] noe hindranc to their service, it was thervpon resolv'd, that eight ships for that purpose should be sent, wch having done that worke should awaite the rest at Plimouth. this being settled by an order of the board, was directed to the Commiſioners of the navie [as] certified by letters to the Countrie, wch thervpon conceavd

Page 132.

good hope & satiffaction, though the sequell did not answear it. thóse Commissioners were the men, that had the great business of that time. the whole strength &/ preparation being navall, they were the masters of it. either for that perticular then in hand or anie other service & designe for the honor, or saftie of the kingdome, wch consisted in those Arks: theyr iudgments & discreations must dispose it. they were first instituted, in the creation of their office vnder the Admiraltie of the E[arl] of Nottingham, for a check & superintendanc to the Admirall, that the whole kingdome stood not toomuch entrusted to one man; but after, through the conversion of the times, they became onlie subservient to the Admirall; his instruments to negotiat his ends, & his obiects against envie; *inani nomine,* as those ministers in Tacitus, *alienæ culpæ pretendebantur;* they had a great power in name, but little libertie to vse it; onlie they were an apt disguise & shadowe & a common ffather for all faults. I obferve this the sooner, to shew the varietie of effects, wch may be emergent from one cause, & how from the same roote & principle, both good & ill derive themfelves. this office, in the inftitution, was wth reason for the common good & benefitt, to rectifie the actions/ of the Admirall (though laterallie it might have some obliquitie) but the execution of it after was soe prestigious & corrupt, as nothing more dangerous & obnoxious. the Admirall had wth them a free command & libertie, whateuer he but intimated they did, & if complaint succeeded it, the error was their owne. of their number the first & principall was Sr John Coke, whom we mentioned before, & this was then his beſt honor and imploiment, the rest were but cyphers vnto him. to him that order of the counſell was deliverd; but he (as not subiect to that authoritie, having greater preparations then in hand, yet not to give them perfection in their kinde, but to sort them to the occasion of his thoughts, & theirs from whom he had them, (w[ch] likewise did affoord more matter of complaint) laies it by w[th]out observanc or accompt, soe as the direction of his Ma[tie], the resolution of the Lords, the expectation of the Countrie were all frustrat by that means. this bred both wonder and distast. that a privat Commissioner of the Navie should presume to oppose an order of the Councell, that that order being fortified by a speciall direction from the/ K[ing] should haue noe more observanc in a matter somuch concerning the publicke good & securitie of the kingdome, it was thought strange & fearfull. enemies at home were more doubted vpon this then those pirats & enemies abroad, w[ch] ielosie was augmented by another act & purpose that had it's preparation in that time; w[ch] was for a consignment to the ffrench of certaine war-lick ships, wth all their apparell & munition to be delivered absolutlie into their hands, w[ch] for aught was knowne might have beene vs'd against themselves, or, as the effect did prove it, made the ruine of their frinds. these were seven great marchant ships, & the Vantgard of the king's, of wch we shall speake heerafter. this note being made onlie by the waie to shew the concurrenc of those things : how ielosies did arise, from what roote the[y] sprang, wch after branch't themselues through the whole

Page 135.

state & kingdøme; & in all things made expression of their fruites.

Page 136.

The first budd putt forth on the first daie at Oxford, wher, according to the adiornment being mett, a complaint was exhibited to the/ Commons of a pardon then granted to a Jesuit whom the towne of Exter had imprisoned. divers circumstances were obferv'd in the aggravation of the fact. first the insolenc of the Jesuit & him that brought the pardon refusing to admitt anie deliberation in the pointe vpon the presenting of the pardon, but requiringe an instant answear from the Maior, & threatning him wth the authorities above, if he delaid the least. then the latitude of the patent, wch implied not onlie a pardon for the present, but in effect an indulgenc more extensive, for the after times to come; for as it commanded the release of his imprisonment, soe it was a *supersedeas* to all officers to impeach him for the future. then that clause, wch in all pardons is requird by the statute. that the delinquent before his freedome & discharge, in all such cases should be bound to the good behaviour wth good sureties, was wholie omitted & left out. then the time likewise was observ'd, in w^{ch}

Page 137.

that grant was made, bearing date the twelvth of / Julie, the next daie after the adiornment made at London, when that generall concession was exprest vpon the petition for religion, that the answear should be reall & not verball. this being held an ill comment on that text, & an vnhappie performanc of that promise, wch likewise was the first, itt being in favor of that order wch is most dangerous in religion, & for a person as obnoxious as his order; the whole house vpon the apprehension of these things assum'd one face of sorrowe wonder it wrought in some, fear generallie in all; the confusion of their thoughts imposd a silenc on their tongues, wch having held awhile, thus at length it brake.

Seneca reports it of an Emperor, that being prest to write for the execution of a man, he vs'd this elegie & complaint, *vtinam nescirem literas;* wishing he knew noe letters, rather then to imploie them to such ends. I may at this time in the like sence assume the like expression for myself, *vtinam nescirem loqui,/* I would I could not speake, soe ther were not this occasion. but the confideration of religion, the honor of the K[ing], the service of this place, require me to deale faithfullie wth my hart, having this libertie of my mouth, freelie to render what I doe conceave, & what I would desire vpon the iudgment of this case. I cannot thinke this issued from the K[ing], or, if it did, that he rightlie vnderstood it. I cannot beleeve he gave his pardon to a Jesuit, & that soe soone vpon his promise vnto vs. his favor perchance was intended to the man, & his qualitie conceald by those that did procure it, who secretlie of themselves might extend it to the order. 'tis not seldome amongst princes such things are drawne from them. they cannot read everie grant that passes them, &, if their leasure serv'd, yet sometimes their confidenc would decline it. Though they are princes they leave not to be men. harts they have still, & affections like to others. & trust will follow wher love has gone be-

Page 138.

fore. therfore/ I doubt this some abuse of ministers, who preferr their owne corruptions before religion or the K[ing]. the time perhaps is not now seasonable to question them ; but yet I would have it search't to know the secrets of it. Let the Lord Keeper be examin'd by what warrant he did issue it ; & that being known let vs see who procur'd it. much may be discover'd in this little ; & from this evill cause some good effects may flowe. the K[ing] when he shall trulie be inform'd, may againe recall his grant. it has an example wth the ffrench, who, in the like, report it of St Lewis, that when a murderer had petition'd him, & receav'd a promise of his pardon, as he was at his religious exercise & devotions, & comming to that it'h psalmes, *beatus est qui facit iustitiam in omni tempore*, he revok't that promise & concession & caus'd the malefactor to be executed. this to a privat murderer that pious prince did doe, howmuch more then may we hope it from our K[ing] vpon this grand traitor to the kingdome ?

infinit is the disproportion of the offences,/ equall the pietie of the princes. therfore what iustice was in that, I cannot doubt in this, when the K[ing] our Saint & Soveraign shall rightlie vnderstand it. to that end my motion shall encline, that we proceed forthwth to the examination of the fact, & that being knowne, then to represent it to his ma^{tie}, wth our petition for some help & redress in this perticular ; & for a generall prevention of the like.

vpon this the king's councell did stand vp to make an extenuation or excuse ; or, as some thought, to divert the disquisition that was mov'd for. they made an acknowledgment of the fact, & of the consequenc it imported, but colord it wth a necessitie of the time, vpon the new marriage of the Q [ueen] & hir suite, wth the ffrench Ambassadors assisting hir. they alledg'd it as a custome of K. James, at the departing of Ambassadors, to make a gratification of that kinde. this, they said, was but a perticular for once, & in that the danger was not much. the answear that was comming to the petition for religion, they assurd would give satiffaction for the generall, & therfore/ desir'd that that scruple might resolve into a hopefull expectation for the future. this had not the success that was intended, but the consideration of the pardon did proceed, wherin it was obiected against that part of the apologie for Ambassadors, that their intervention in such cases, was one of the greivances of that time. & theron 'twas observ'd that noe other State admitted it ; nor could the presenc of their prince release one man in Spaine. the infelicitie also of their treaties was then noted, & a large discourse made on it, by that learned and grave gentleman Sr Henry Marten. he shewd that in former times, when ould Ambassadors were imploid whose wisdomes & experience might give a promise for their workes, success did prove it not the proprietie of their nation, as the ffrenchmen likewise, & others had observ'd it. that the dexteritie of Englishmen was in fighting, not in treating, and by that manie millions had been gain'd, as then exhausted by the other. he concluded in the generall, that ther might be sought also a remedie for this, wch causd a sharp reflex vpon him from the envie of the State,/ those that were then in favor taking it for an aspersion on their persons; the Ambassadors wch had treated wth the ffrench then for the marriag of the Q [ueen] being the Duke, the E. of Holland & the E. of Carlile. the first two young & gamesome, fitter for sports then businefs; theother soe ceremonious & affected, that his iudgment & realitie was in doubt, & his aptness conceavd more to have beene *deliciarum arbiter*, as Petronius, then *arbiter regni*, or *negotiis regis*, as Pallas vnder Nero: thefe did take that note of ould Ambassadors to have a contrarie reflection vpon them, wch wth out doubt was signified; &, for this, they were incenst against him, wherof he had not long after a full taste. ther was in that gentleman, great years, great knowledg, great experienc, and great abilities of nature to support them. he was a Doctor of the Lawe, & had almost all the civill iurifdiction in his hands, being Judge of the Admiraltie, Judge of the prerogative, Judge of the Arches. in the first he stood as an officer to the Duke, but the cheife dutie he profest was to Justice, & his Countrie. this was the first parliament he had servd in, this almost his first entrance to the/ Parliament, this the first triall of his service, wch had such a reward from the Court, as might have beene a discouragment to some other, & was not w^thout trouble vnto him. but in the house it had a good approbation & acceptance, as it did speake that truth, wch was written on each hart; & the generall being laid vp for some other opportunitie, the perticular was refolv'd on to be followd by a petition to the K[ing]. & a Committee to that end appointed to prepare it.

this was the agitation of the first daie, and the next daie had the like; when, after the first reading of some bills, as the vsuall manner is before the house be full for the entertaynment of the morning, the cause of Mountague was resum'd & the last order read, vpon wch he stood committed. the Sariant thervpon being requird to bring his prisoner to the barr, anfweard that he had left him sicke, & by a letter from him was advertisd that his weakness was such as he could not travell, wch giving noe satiffaction to the house, that thought it an excuse, divers expressions were [used] vpon [it], shewing a difaffection to the man. & that his letter was held delatorie/ to avoid the question of his works, wch being made an aggravation to his faults, rais'd the confideration of his punishment to the greater severitie & heigth; & therfor it was vrg'd that he should presentlie be sent for. this the king's Sollicitor did oppose by intimating a message from the K[ing] that he was a chaplaine in ordinarie to his ma^{tie}, & that his ma^{tie} had taken that cause into his care, wch would appeer vpon his answear to the petition for religion. therfor he prest for a message to the K[ing] to importune him for a remedie therin, wch he doubted not, would be granted to the full satiffaction of their harts, much trouble being sav'd, and yet the worke accomplish't. this was thought rather a diversion then advise, & a waie conducing to some new preiudice & danger, noe safe retreat or issue out of that.

Page 144.

it was replied that answears were but words, & their satiffaction was not much wher deeds did contradict them. as Mountague was said to be then a chaplaine to the K[ing] it was obiected, as a note, for dissuasion to that waie, in what time he was made soe. in the beginning of the Parliament he was a stranger to/ the Court, receav'd but since his question, & whether or noe, on that occasion, it was doubtfull, as what protection it might render. therfore that Councell of going by petition was dislik't. it was said to be vnparliamentarie, as vnfafe; but the other *more maiorum*, & iuridicall. that extraiudiciall courses, to that house had beene seldome fortunat & auspitious, of wch some precedents were instanc't, as the like remission to K. J[ames] of the causes of Ireland & Virginia 18° of his raigne. & that of Sr Symon Harby 21°. that all Justices & deputie leiftenants in the Counties, this being granted, may haue the like priviledg & protection. naie it was alledg'd further that noe man could committ a publicke crime or iniurie; but by color of some publicke imploiment for the K[ing] & soe all being made his servants, as that was then requir'd, all, by the same reason should be free from the iurisdiction of the Parliament. what the Parliaments would be then, & what the Countrie by such Parliaments, was offerd to the consideration of the howse, wth a strong caution on that pointe to be carefull for posteritie. it was added that the/ K[ing] ought not to take knowledg of their acts, before they were made publicke & represented by the house. that the examples of all times did warrant their intentions, & all qualities of men had beene subiect to their questions, as the D. of Gaunt & the Lo. Latimer 50 E. 3 were ther impeacht for giving ill counsell to the K[ing]. noe Dukedome or greatness could exempt them from the iurisdiction of that Court, & the right was still the same. the case of S' Thomas Parrie was remembred 12° Ja[mes] for whom being a Councellor of State the K[ing] then by like message interpos'd : but the priviledg of the house was a direction to that time, wch proceeded vnto iudgment, & gave sentenc in the case. by these reasons was supported the refolution to proceed notwthstanding the king's message. the voge went generallie as it was mov'd at first, that he should presentlie be fent for ; but this having a little alteration in the forme, for that he stood committed to the sariant, and therfore should be taken, as in custodie, & a prisoner. the Sariant was thervpon commanded to produce him, or at his perill to answear the neglect. some in this dispute had sallied vpon/ the confideration of his books, & therin tooke occasion to argue his opinions, descending into the subtilties of the fchoolemen, about the infallibility of grace, the antecedent & confequent wills of God ; but their zeale being more commended then their iudgment, those doctrinall points were wav'd, as not proper subiects for that place, & the dispute was carried onlie vpon the consideration of his person.

this difficultie being over, a new one did arise of the same kinde though differing in the forme. Dr Anian one of the masters of the colledges, who had likewise beene question'd by that Court, was appointed then to preach before both houses the next Sundaie. this was thought an affront vnto the Parliament. the burgesses of that Vniversitie were cal'd for. these were sent to [the] vice-chancelor to expostulat the fact. the Vice-chancelor speaking wth Anian, returnd his answear that he would not desift. but in observance to the house he after causd the delegats to meet, who difchargd him from the service, & nam'd another in his stead, making wth some difficultie an accommodation in that pointe. this shewd/ likewise the spirit of that partie, w[ch] studied an innovation in the church, & was taken for an indication of more danger. that bouldness thought improper for such men, schollers & churchmen being not alwaies found soe confident. still it increast the fear, & wth that, the ielosie grew more hott, w[ch] then appeerd in sparks, & after flam'd more cleerlie.

Page 148.

Both houses heer againe, it being the generall daie appointed for the kingdome, concurr'd in the celebration of the fast. the outward pietie seem'd great, & manie, doubtless, had it trulie in their harts. yet some insinceritie was suspected wher the practise & professions did not meet; that holinefs being distrusted, w[ch] ha's not righteousness to accompanie it. the next morning, by a message from the K[ing] both houses were commanded to attend him presently at christ church. wher, after some little expectation, his ma[tie] being come, he begann wth the occafion of that meeting, & some short expressions of himself. somewhat he toucht of the preparation then in hand, & the necessitie of the worke, wth a remembranc of their ioynt & mutuall ingagements/ thervnto, saying, that better it

Page 149.

were half his ships should perish, then that the ffleet should not goe foorth. he vrg'd also, in his manner, the expenc that had beene made, & wthout a further ayd that ther was an impossibilitie to proceed. some intimation he vf'd likewise of the guift that had beene past, & his acceptanc, but not satiffaction on that pointe. concluding wth a consideration of the time how dangerous it was, & leaving it to the iudgment of that Councell, whether they would hould greater, the fear of the sickness to themfelves, or the difhonor of their nation. Somewhat he added for the answear to the petition of religion. that wthin two daies they should have it, wch as a cordiall & restaurative was then given to sweeten the operation of the rest.

this was seconded by the Secretarie of State the Lo. Conwey, who reckoninge vp perticulars of the charge, the same that had beene formerly & afterwards were manie times repeated, making an immence calculation of ye treasures soe exhausted, wherin, he said, ther wanted some thirtie or fowrtie thousand pownds to doe the worke, the officers being difcredited by the sickness, & wthout w^{ch}/ the ffleet could not goe out. the warr, he alledgd, was occasiond by the Parliament in the counsell wch they gave for the dissolution of the treaties. in that confisted the honor of the kingdome, the saftie of religion, & the generall good of christendome. if the preparations should dissolve, he said, the Germans would divide, the ffrench disband, & revnite them to the Catholicks, the K[ing] of Denmarke retire & make his peace wth the Emperor, who, wth the D[uke] of Savoy & the Venetians were drawn by K[ing]

Page 150.

J[ames] into the League, wch difficulties being foreseene, the K[ing] therfore resorted to his subiects to crave that help from them, wch his ancestors in like cases had receavd. this was the summe of that wch he deliverd, being but the abstract of that wch was to come; for heer againe were vs'd those great abilities of Sr John Coke, on whom the weight of that burden was impos'd; who, though yet noe publicke minister of the State, & a member of the Commons, was w^th'out leave from them, & that never done by anie man before, in their presenc made a dictator for the K[ing]. & after some formalitie of seeming to take inftructions at the present, in that wch he had studied long before, having the honor in the face of that assemblie/ to be cal'd vp privatlie to the State, & from thenc returning, as from an Oracle inspir'd wth a new spirit & wisdome, thus he propounds those sacred reasons he had gather'd for the occasion of that time. his beginning was at the end of the Spanish treaties, wherein he shew'd, that the late K[ing] at the instance of the Parliament, by the cooperation of his ma^tie that then was, & the D. of Buckingham (giving them that coniunction) was drawne to breake wth Spaine. that he thervpon considering the troubles that must follow it, ther being no other means but warr for recoverie of the Pallatinat, & to moderat the greatness of that K. whose forces then possest it, &, vnder color of the Catholicke cause & league, aspir'd to make himself a Catholicke prince & Monarck. & foreseeing the dangers of that change, in respect of the qualitie of his people, through a long peace & quiet become vnapt for warr, at

least in much want of art & preparation, he prudentlie
dissembled his intentions for a while, that others, by the
discoverie of his purpose, made not advantage thervpon ;
& suffer'd himself to be entertaind wth mediations &
entreaties, & new propositions to be made him, vntill by
degrees he/ came to that wch he intended, nothing being   Page 152.
omitted in the *interim* that might settle his affaires. the
Pallatinat he sawe divided by his enemies, & held, *de facto*,
by their powers. a Dyet likewise cal'd to invest them wth
the right, & to exclude all hope of restitution. In ffrance
he sawe all things in combustion, & the K[ing] ther
inclining to sheath his sword in the bowells of his subiects,
rather then to turne it against others; & the Low Countries
in great danger & necessitie by the potencie of their adversaries, & the faction of the Arminians, wch begann to
make an interruption in their goverment, & threat'ned
them in more. these things weigh'd, for an encouragment
to the States, he lent them 6000 men, & paie for their
entertaynment for two years. &, to make the more strick't
coniunction wth the ffrench, sought their alliance for his
sonne, & by that match to make the bond inviolable
between them. the German princes & the K[ing] of
Denmarke he sollicited, whose couldness was immoveable
vntill they should see his ma^{tie} in the feild. the charge for
that being cast, what a land armie would require, & the
computation rising to 700,000^{li} p anñ his ma^{tie} in contem-
plation/ of his people ; thought of some thriftier course, &   Page 153.
to that end drew a league betweene ffrance, Savoy, Venice,
the low countries, & himself, for the raising of 30000.

foot, & 6000. horse, to serve vnder the Command of Count Mansfeilt, he being to contribute to that charge but 20000^{li} a month. this being done, & a preparation likewise of his fleet, the K. of Denmarke thervpon comming into the League promis'd to raise a great armie in those parts, for wch the K[ing] alfo was to contribut 30000^{li} amonth. these things thus setled by K[ing] J[ames] being in preparation, or in act, the fruite wherof is yet shadowed vnder hope, his ma^{tie} not willing to desert it, being the effect of the Councell given by Parliament, by Parliament he desir'd to follow & accomplish it. wch requiring a more charge then his treasures will supplie, ther being 40000^{li} disburst alreadie for the navie, wch is now vpon the Seas going towards the Rendezvous at Plimouth, wher ther be 10000 landmen for the action wch ha's soe great an expectation in the world; ther wants yet some monie to supplie them, some necessaries for the ships, some provisions for the men, wthout wch neither can be serviceable. it is the first fruits/ of our warfare, the *primitiæ* of the K. wherin the hope of our allies, the interests of religion, the honor of the kingdome are ingag'd, wch shews that this Parliament was not cald meerlie vpon formalitie after the accession to the Crowne, but for the consultation of this business, that as the Parliament did beginne, the Parliament might end it. thus spake that oracle. besides he added that his Matie had intelligence of a designe to trouble Ireland, & an increase of the enemies navie in the Low Countries, wth a purpose to thrust over part of their Armies into England: but as noe king was more loving to his subiects, soe his ma^{tie} was confident, that noe subiects were more loving to their K[ing]. & therfore he left it wholie to their choise, whether, by ballancing the occasions, they should think fitter, vpon the consideration of the time, to let the Action fall, or to give him more releife. this was the summe of his expression, somewhat more large, but to this sence & purpose. & further he made this postill vpon that perticular of Mansfeilt in apologie & excuse, that though it had not answeard the expectation at the full, yet it had produc'd/ some fruits worthie of that designe, as the putting off of the Dyett in Germanie, the encouragment of the princes, the comming of the K. of Denmark into the feild, the attempts of the ffrench vpon Millaine, the reconciliation of the ffrench protestants & their K[ing], & the scattering of the enemies forces in the Low countries, in wch some things being more then his last difcourse on the same subiect did containe, it was thought to be more studied not more true, nothing either of intelligenc or fact having happened in that time, to give it other color then his fancie. the rest being in substance but what he had said before, & a repetition in effect of his proposition made at London, had not much obfervation for the matter, though some passages were more noted, wch then did open, & give discoverie to the secret. both in the king's discourse & his, the conclusion was not iudg'd answearable to the premises. the referring of the action at that time, advanc't to soe much forwardness, was not conceiv'd agreeable wth the pretended importanc of the worke, wherin such treasures

Page 155.

had beene spent. the calculations that were made argued the necessitie/ of the thing, wth out wch infinit preparations would not be, & the *equilibrio* it was left in, made it but adiaphorall. the interpretations were various wch it had, according to the fancies that they came from. those that were more charitable did inferr, that, ther being some speciall service first intended, the opportunitie had prevented it, & soe the designe was lost. thofe that possest more ielosie did collect, that a secret reconciliation had beene made; &, by some privat treatie & convention, a composition and agreement of all difference. but all beleev'd the preparation should be left; noe ships nor men to be drawne further in the imploiment; & that the studie was how to impute it to the Parliament, either their counfell or deniall to be an occasion to dissolve it; some color onlie sought for the satisfaction of the world, that what ever did occurr, a cause might be in readiness, &, if the reason pres't it, a faire excuse at hand. But the summe mov'd for seem'd a miracle, wch had it's confideration after wth the Commons, wher the treaties & mediations that were spoken of, & that speaker's act it self came into question & dispute; & that paralell,/ & coniuncture of cooperation wth the K. was not, though silenc't, yet forgotten. the next daie was the entranc to that sceane, the remayne of that being reserv'd for meditation, when all the members of the Commons speciallie appointed to attend, having resolvd the overtures that were made, a Lawier first beginns, as a prologue to the act, drawing his considerations for the conclusion of the K[ing]. that the K[ing] having left it indifferentlie to their choife (ballancing the importanc of his service, wth the dangers of the time) whether they would sitt to thinke of a new supplie, or part and lose the action ; he desir'd first that ther might be a conferenc wth the Lords to learne, if they could tell it, whether the confequenc were such of the preparations then in hand, as it was more in relation to the kingdome, then the saftie of their lives. if soe that then he was noe Englishman that would leave it ; to die refolutlie for their Countrie, having beene the honor of their nation; if otherwise, that he was noe frind to England that desir'd it, nor could they, in wisdome, give them selves as a sacrifice to their enemies. the K[ing] he said,/ had gratiouslie refer'd it vnto them, & they, Page 158. in dutie to the K[ing] ought to resolve it prudentlie. the greater good must be preferd. fancie & affection must not governe in such counsells. that the probabilitie seem'd against sitting at that time, the supplie wch was demanded being too little for their valewes, less then they should spend, if they continued ther awhile. but the better to determine it, he wisht ther might be a conferenc wth the Lords. they had like interest in the sitting, their dangers being equallie involvd, though the supplies were onlie the proprietie of the Commons ; therfore he mov'd the house to goe presentlie to them, & soe by a ioynt advise mutuallie to conclude.

this introduction was not lik't by those that had relation to the Court, it declining wholie the course of their affections ; and to that end some obiections it receav'd & some diversions followd them. it was alledgd to be vnparliamentarie & improper, vpon a proposition from the K[ing] to seeke an interpretation from the Lords, who might be as ignorant as others, & could not iudge the worth of what they knew not ; nor would discretion soe presume, though it might know a part to fett/ an estimat on the whole. it was mov'd likewise that they should first state the propositions that were made, & soe by *capita* debate them : but that leading into a laborinth & Meander, wher nothing but confusion could be found, was left, as that expeld the former, in the roome of wch another did arise, whose spirit, once vp, was not soe eafily coniur'd downe. this came from S^r ffrancis Seymor who wth much bouldness, & some asperitie did deliuer it. Laying it for a ground, vpon that meeting & assemblie, that ther could be noe other end therof, then the corrupt purposes of some, to putt a ielosie & dissention betweene their Soveraigne & his subiects. the proposition he divided, & soe answear'd, that for monie, wch was the first part, as the K[ing] had beene content wth their first grant at London, if more should then be given it could not be levied till the spring, when the other subsidies might be past, & against that time they might have mett againe. for credit, the second part, wch might be pretended by a grant he said, it was an argument to the difhonor of the K[ing], kings having more in the generall affection of their subiects, then anie perticullar diclaration/ could implie, this making them but entitled to a part, the other to the whole, what ever his subiects did possess, as ther was occasion for his service. it were, he said, too great a shew of wante & povertie in the State, to suppose that small summe nam'd, wch he did blush to thinke of, needed a parliament to procure it. wher is the ould treasure of the kingdome, the reputation of the state, that the times of Q. El[izabeth] enioy'd, when the least of manie ministers of hirs, if ther had beene occasion, could, of his owne creditt, have supplied a greater summe then this? & when that famous princes[s] never to be forgotten, having noe wante, nor vse, onlie in prevention of hir enemies, tooke vp at once of the ffoulkers then in Germanie almost all the coyne of christendome? wher is this credit now? wher are those ministers in this age? I doubt their worth & fidelitie is gone. that they are the men wch bring this necessitie to their master; that they have exhausted thus his treasures, spent his revenewes, & being conscious of these faults, by the vnnecessarie preparations they have caus'd, now seeke to color it by some others, &, if they can, to laie the blame on vs./ wee have been tould of late of a peace in ffrance & a reconciliation for the protestants, but who knows not the present violenc against them? & we may wishe therin that our ships doe not impeach them. ther were five subsidies & three fifteenths not long since given for the Q[ueen] of Bohemia & that service, but what has shee beene better'd? what has beene therw^th done worthie of that intention? noe enemie is declar'd; nothing has been attempted but the consumption of our selves. thus he said, vsing besides some generall notes of princes; if their happinefs that were councel'd by men of worth & knowledg, & the contrarie wher they rest vpon confidenc of some few, that can but begg, or flatter. vpon w^ch

Page 161.

he resum'd againe the memorie of the Q[ueen] who was munificent to hir servants, but from hir owne stores, not feeding them on the marrow of hir subiects. & he concluded that he doubted not to see the like greatness in the K[ing] if he would give them leave to doe somewhat for the Countrie wherby they might be enabled & encourag'd to yeeld him seasonable supplie, & for whose service noe dangers could deterr them. this being another/ pitch, & to another pointe directed then the former, some wisht againe for that, & in the grave therof this other to be buried. the courtiers sawe themselves encounter'd in their waie, & their desire of sitting then purfued, though in affection vnto them, not to their end & purpose. that charge vpon the ministers of State, the sallie on their councells, the paralell of the times, was noe good musicke in their eares, wth wch all mention of the elders had antipathie, & the glories of that princess were like basalisks in their eyes. that note of flatterie and begging also was knowne to have reflection on the favorits ; & that bouldness gaue suspition of yet more : to prevent w^{ch}, & the storme was like to follow it, the chancelor of the Dutchie did stand vp & vs'd these reasons & perswasions. that if the plate & iewells of the K[ing] or the plate & iewells of some others whom he heard dasht vpon, could have procur'd monie at that time, they had not mett ther then. things he said were turn'd fairlie to advantage, making therin an insinuation for those persons, to whose meritt he imputed it, not naming anie, but leaving it not doubted whom he meant. when the Parliament did/ advise the dissolution of the treaties, he alledgd, a warr was then expected, from wch common place he argued the dangers they were in. ffrance & Spaine vnited, both in allianc & affection, & the Pope still labouring to endear them; for the supportation of his cause. the Germans then broken by the Emperor. the K[ing] of Denmarke a warie prince vnlikelie to ingage himself in warr for the benefit of others. yet such was the conversion of the time, as ffrance & Spaine were seperat. that two armies were levied by the ffrench & one march't into the Valtoline, theother against Genoa. the Germans revnited. the Dane prepar'd for warr; all wch did follow vpon the declaration of K[ing] J[ames] in the setting foorth of Mansfeilt, the next daie after the shipping of his men at Douer the ffrench beginning wth their armies then to march; soe as the rest of the English preparations were expected, ther being presum'd a confidenc vpon that; & if that credit should be lost, besides the disadvantage of the worke, it would be a generall loss to the honor of the nation, & impeach the reputation & esteeme/ wch is the sowle & life of everie state & goverment. he vrg'd againe that the King's ingagement was by them, & that he vndertooke but the designes wch they propounded; & thervpon he inferd that the Parliament ought not to receed; that if the success were ill, other men might be furnisht wth excuses, & the misfortune imputed to that house for not supplying necessaries. this he enforc't further wth an example of those times, or next them, wch he said, were soe pretious in their memories, when the E. of Devonshire, not at his instance or his frinds, was sent

Page 164.

deputie into Ireland, & the Spanish armie landing, & ther ioyning wth the rebells, to the hasard of the kingdome, wherin happne'd that difficult siege of Kingsale, he was still furnish't from the Court, though by his enemies, wth all things necessarie for that service, & when it came into the deliberations of the Councell, the E. of Salifburie then Tresurer by way of protestation did affirme, that he could not complaine of them; nothing had beene wanting of their help, & if ther were a miscarriage in the action, the blame muft be his/ owne. from thenc he drew a perswasion for the like that they should then accord to make supplie, & soe laie the burden vpon others. he concluded wth an apothegme, wherof he was never wth out store, that monie given in that house might be caft into the Sea, & soe some treasure lost; but not given, posteritie might rue it, reservation in such cases being more dangerous then adventure. the witt of this gentleman alwaies drew the attention of the house, though his motions seldome relisht it. the observation wch he made vpon the E. of devonshire was thought true, though the application were not proper, & his note, but a fallacie, for the time. his intelligenc was knowne good in the passages of that sceane, having been a servant to that E. bred vnder his command, & wth him in those troubles: but his relations in other things were doubted, as his vrging of the ingagment was dislik't, & generallie his intentions had a preiudice as comming from the Court. yet some scruples he had raisd by that difcourse & argument. the desire & expectation of deniall, wch most men did beleeve,

seem'd to have a contradiction by his/ waie, pressing soe Page 166.
directlie for supplie, he being noe stranger to the cabanet.
this caus'd a diftraction in some thoughts, that by the
superficies iudg'd the bodie: but those that tooke the de-
mension of all parts, in the depth therof, found another
sence & meaning, wch was, but to qualifie the ielosie conceav'd & to divert that confideration of the Councells, w^{ch}
he perceavd, having a sharp iudgment & inspection, had
inflam'd the affection of the house, that noe small matter
could allay it; opposition being like fewell to such fiers, &
therfore he indeavor'd it, by changing that suppos'd state
ot'h cause, that soe, if possible, he might change the order
in proceeding. & to endear this further, another of his
fellow counfellors & officers, the Tresurer of the houfhold,
did second him wth a perticular proposition for two subsidies; but that labor was in vaine, the quarrell being
begunne; all men were apprehensive of the iniurie, &
manie did express it. soe hard it is, wher publicke wrongs
are done, to keep them from vindication, or complaint.
minions may enioy the favor of their masters, but if they
once abuse it, noe priviledg can protect them. the subiects/
crie will follow them, & if it prevaile not vpon earth, Page 167.
heaven will hear & help them. iustice is provided for their
adverfaries, seldome they scape it heer, neuer heerafter, but
vengeanc does attend them, wch should make them more
cautious in offending, when the offences done are soe
hardlie left vnpunished. that meeting might have beene
prevented wth much saftie; but being mett, that crime was
thought vnpardonable. he that was the occasion of that

trouble, must have his share therin, & by that means of more, till the measure of his iniquities was full, & then vengeance must surprise him like a whirlewind, & noe favor or greatness may deliver him, but, as his meritt such must be his reward. But to resume our storie. the proposition of those counsellors for supplie had but a could acceptanc, & the intention wch it carried to divert the former motions was wholie reiected & in vaine; & thus those motions were pursued in a high straine of eloquenc by that master of expression Sr Robert Phelips, who casting his notions into a quadripartite division, for method & order to his speach, in more then wonted gravitie, to raise

Page 168. the expectation of his hearers/ having compos'd himself, thus he propounds his sence. ffirst for the meeting (wch was the first member of his division) he said it was to him not inferior to a miracle, ther having beene at London such satiffaction in their works, as noe servant of the kings, nor minister of State, (if they must be diftinguish't) but approv'd what they had done ; & his ma^tie himself, who was more then thousands others, gave such an acknowledgment therof, as the adiornment was resolv'd, in counterpoife of that, for the preservation of their healths, wch he did ballanc equallie wth the consideration of his owne. this having beene the satiffaction of that time, nothing occurring after for the change or alteration that was made ; noe new enemie discover'd, nor newe designe in hand, noe new danger pressing it, how thofe new councells should be taken, how that should seeme too little wch was then thought enough, how that satiffaction should be lost, & by that their favor wth his ma^tie, noe reason, he said, could resolve him on that pointe, nothing but divinitie could iudge. that, it was a strange president they had mett, when vpon the declaration of his ma^tie, & his acceptance of that guift, moſt of their members being retir'd, & soe few left that they could be hardlie cal'd a house, that then/ a proposition should be made, like a sur- Page 169. prise of enemies, not as an overture from frinds, who should deale cleerlie & aboue board, not circumvent the innocent, not make such requitall of their loves. this, he observ'd, was the action of that gentleman who, he said, did that yesterdaie, wch was never done before; & for both deserv'd to render an accompt, for though the danger were avoided in the former, the attempt was not the less; & for the latter, noe reason could excuse it. that those things were strange, but the adiornment, & that meeting ther farr more, to have the whole kingdome hurried in such hast for the will & pleasure of one subiect (for it could not be the K[ing] should have such mutibilitie in himself): that that subiect should presume to tranffer his errors to the Parliament, that the Parliament should be thought a fitt ffather for great faults, this, he profest, was beyond all example & comparison, hardlie the former president of that place could be a match therin; the first danger in accession being less, the proiect & intention not worse, & in respect therof, it being but iustice to desire it that the success & issue, for what concern'd/ those ministers, were the same. Page 170. that therfore he was not of opinion wth those that would not sitt. that he valued not his saftie wth the saftie & welfare of the kingdome. that god having brought them thither, as Joseph went for Egipt, by that comming, though vnwisht for, some glorious worke might be. what was not intended amongst men, providenc & divinitie could induce; they were to act their parts & leaue the success to god.

this was his expression on that part. the next concern'd the councells of the kingdome, wherein reflecting vpon the Spanish laborinth & treaties, he said, that god had made it a nationall punishment for their sinns. that by that treaty was induc'd that dangerous iorney of their prince, led on by the flattering counsells of those servants who had brought K[ing] J[ames] in love wth the deceiptfull face of frindship, & betraied him to the netts of those subtile, foxlike, artificiall faithless people; as he then termd the Spaniards. he remembred what was suffered in that cause, for the opposition made in Parliament 18° of that raigne, when/ he said, their liberties were harased; their persons in restraint, of wch he had borne a share by the ill influenc of those planets, being tax't for nothing, but speaking against that match. of wch difasters being free, both in the generall & perticular by a cause stranger then the effect, that iorney into Spaine, wch begann not to that end, that three things in the next parliament were desir'd & promisd, but scarce kept. the first, for prevention in the future, that noe more such treaties might endanger them, but the prince to match wth one of his owne religion. the second, that there might be such respect vnto our neighbours, as to preserve their safties, who were reciprocallie a saftie vnto them. the third, to maintaine the religion in the kingdome, that the lawes might have their life, & not delinquents be suffered to affront them. how those were kept, that, the certaintie was too great. what were the Spanish articles 'twas knowne, what then the ffrench 'twas doubted. that papists did still increase, their priefts & Jesuits grow more bould, little being done for support of the allies,/ a profest couldness even in all, & by what councells it was soe, both truth & reason spake. ffor the present state & condition of the people, wch was the third branch of his divifion, he deduc'd a demonftration from septimo of K[ing] J[ames] & remembred the question of imposing then on foote, & the title of prerogative therin. how it was then handled in that house, argued, & debated for the interests of the subiect, & resolvd to be their right, their inheritanc to be free, & yet the fact continuinge in preiudice of that libertie. how in 12°. itt was resum'd, distributed into parts, & a conference thervpon intended wth the Lords, soe by a message sought, but, through the practise of some ministers refus'd, & all papers after taken wch had relation to that business, & the records & bookes, wch had the evidenc of those liberties, burnt & consum'd, wth the liberties themselves, as farr as present power could rule the iudgment of posteritie. Since wch time, ther having beene a large bountie of the subiect, as two subsidies 18°. three subsidies & fifteenths given in the last parliament of K[ing] J[ames] onlie wth a claime for continuation in that pointe, & the manie/ disputes declin'd ; yet that soe little had that bountij or modestie prevail'd, as

Page 172.

Page 173.

the effect of that greivanc was still on them, &, that wch never was before, the tonnage & pondage levied & collected wth out a graunt from them, as if right were an impertinenc to States, wher power & force are extant. by wch ther had been more pressures on the people wth in the space of seven years then last past, than, almost, in seven ages next before it. this, he said, for the subiect, in part might shew the condition he was in, what abilitie was left him, what affection he might have. besides from the consideration of the State, he said, ther came as small encouragment. that councells were ther monopoliz'd, as the generall liberties elswher. that the whole wisdome was supposd to be comprehended in one man. that he being master of the favor, was likewise master of all business. *nihil vnquam prisci & integri moris*, as Tacitus notes in the declination of the Romans, *sed exuta a'qualitate omnia vnius iussa aspectare.* though ther were manie councellors in name, that few retaind the dignitie *æquales ordinis, magis quam operis*, as Paterculus has it of the like, though their reputation might be somewhat, yet that their/ authoritie was but small, & their affections asmuch captiv'd as their greatness. this he did make an argument that god was not their frind. that by those abuses of favor amongst men, they had lost the favor of the almightie. that he was become their enemie, & vnless they had peace wth him, in vaine it was to thinke of warr wth others. that therfore an inward preparation must precead, before those outward preparations could be hopefull, the watchman waking but in vaine if the Lord watch not wth him. further he said, it was a

Page 174.

strong argument of the sickness of the State, when the credit was soe weake, as it was then pretended, that it could not wth out a parliament take vp 40000^{li} wch was a could perswasion then to give, when such men were soe neer, who were the causes of it. that though it were impossible for the supposition to take place, that the English shuld leave their K[ing] yet in respect of this great abuse of Counsells, if anie man made a stand, the blame muſt light on those that had occasiond it, whom, for securitie in that case, it was therfore fitt, after the examples of ther ffathers, the parliament/ should indeavor to remove. from thenc he descended to his fourth & last perticular, wch was his opinion on the whole, wherin vsing againe some touches of the former contention in that place though not approving the diforders but commending the reformation that was sought for, he concluded for an imitation in that pointe ; not that he would have them tread soe neer the heeles of maiestie, yet, not to suffer all things by that name. as the K[ing] was wrongd in the iniurie of his subiects, he said, it was their dutie to vindicat them both. that he would not have them reason of what they vnderstood not, whether the ffleet shuld goe or staie, not knowing the designe. that the eſtate at home, the affaires civill & domesticke were the proper obiects of their cares : to settle the goverment of the kingdome, rectifie the disorders, reforme the grave abuses, heale the difease therof. that these were their business & for this he would not have them thinke of parting, but be suitors to his ma^{tie} that he would giue them time to sitt, in this great service for him,

Page 175.

wch would afford him a more ample aid & credit, then manie subsidies could give; the/ streames of his revenewes being cleerd, those scattred beames collected, his exhaust stores replenisht, the fountaine of his checker fil'd againe, & all this wth the love & satiffaction of his subiects. this he desir'd might be the resolution of that house, & for that address to the K[ing] a Committee to prepare it. this raisd the difaffection that was movd to a greater heigth & sharpness; & not onlie the iniurie of that meeting was then lookt att, but the whole preiudice of the time; all the miffortunes that were suffred, both forraigne & domesticke were imputed to those ministers, who vsurpt that power of greatness, & by abuse of the favor of their prince drew all things to their wills. against this prodigious greatness, wch like a comet was suspected to threaten great difasters to the kingdome, the generall intention of that house beganne then to be inflam'd, &, neither parting nor supplie were thought confiderable in the case, but the reformation that was spoken of, the restauration of the goverment. to stop wch streame & currant another of the privie councellors stood up, Sr Richard Weston chancelor of the Exchecker, who practif'd then for others what he must after indeavor for himself, such/ being the fatalitie of great persons, as example of misfortunes cannot move them. this man must see in others what were the dangers of exorbitance, how Phaeton rose & fell, wanting a moderation to containe him, yet honor and ambition must transport him, let ffortune rule the rest. to the present purpose first he applied some short answears to that wch was vrg'd before;

for religion saying that he doubted not the satiffaction would be speedie, & noe more fear in that : for the councells, he excus'd them wth the long time of peace, that had bred some errors in the State by a dependance vpon treaties, wch follow'd the inclination of K[ing] J[ames] & might then be rectified by their advice vnto that K[ing] : yet in somethings he said, he might iustifie their works; & theron mentiond the Leagues that had beene spoken of, & the effects pretended, wth the advantage vnder hope. from whenc he paft to positive reasons of his owne, for that seeming perswasion of supplie. the first was drawne from the necessity of the worke, the honor of the kingdome, the restitution of their frinds, the cause of religion being in it, & the generall good of christendome, all the princes as he pretended being ingag'd, to hate & love &/ fear at once wth them, who as they warm'd would coole, if they had their example. the next was from the necessitie of the K[ing] who by the expences of his ffather, had his chests emptied, his revenewes all anticipated, his debts great, & for the supportation of his charge, wch besides the preparation then in hand, was not little towards the funerall, Ambassadors & the like, for wch he was faine to take vp monies of the citie vpon the pawne and morgage of his lands. another was taken from the dangers of division if the[y] should part abruptlie. the K[ing] he said in Spain had obfervd the preiudice wch his ffather had therin, how the homebred ielosies & diftractions, betweene his subiects & himself had brought him to contempt, wch he therfore in his person had the last parliament indeavor'd as a happie starr & planett by his sweet influenc to compose, as knowing, that the contrarie cause, must have a like contrarie effect; by wch parliament came more grace vnto the people in the happie lawes then past, then at anie time before; wherin ther being soe reall a demonstration of his virtues, he alledgd, that ought then to gaine him trust, as those/ other reasons likewise drawne from the occafion & necessitie, to prevaile for the supplie. what ever were after done, he added, that action must be then, that the affaires abroad were not to be commanded, other things might staie. the expectation of the world being vpon that first action of the K[ing] if he loft then his honor, that it was noe small thing he parted wth, it being the honor also of the nation, wch had noe medium betweene their glorie & their shame. that the fruit of their former labors was in that, & if they ther should leave it, both that & all their bounties were in vaine; & not confirming then the counfells they had given, beyond that daie ther was noe place for Councell. soe he concluded, & that other questions being wav'd that onlie might be spoken to, wherin he concurr'd wth the proposition of his fellow for two subsidies & two fifteenths, rather as 'twas thought to ioyne in some perticular then by inftruction, for the summe. for it was noted to varie from that speech, wch was made before the K[ing]. wherin thirtie or fortie thousand pounds was talk't of; but this perhaps was but to hasten the deniall the sooner by enlarging the demande, wch was confidered in the replies/ that followed, wth that strange clause of limitation to their councells, wherin less being deem'd of prophecie then menace, the dislike it mov'd was greater then the fear, wch quickning still the humor that was stir'd, drew this expression further from that great ffather of the Lawe Sr Edward Coke, who in much observanc to the house, much respect vnto the cause, having consulted wth his memorie of the proceedings in like cases, from the presidents of the Antients made this introduction & beginninge.

that 37 E[dward] 3. when that prudent warlike K[ing] was in the exaltation of his glorie, & yet the subiects suffred through the abuses of some ministers, the Commons then petitiond him to command his Bishops & clergie to praie for three things, the State & happiness of his ma^tie, the peace & good goverment of the kingdome, & the preservation & continuanc of virtue & love betweene his subiects & himself, wch they then said, were all hasarded by his officers & vntill their remove, noe subventions could be made. this, he show'd, was at that time wth out iniurie or diftast, & the same reason was for them, in confidence whereof, he said, he would freelie speake his hart, for the honor of his soveraigne, not doubting but his goodness would soe take it. after this preamble/ he made division of the question, reducing it to this, whether they should then make an addition of supplie, or how otherwise to give subfistence to his ma^tie. to wch points he addrest his subsequent difcourse, that being a superstruction on this building. ffor the first he rendred his opinion, not to give, because to ingraft subsidies vpon subsidies was not parliamentarie, & what should be granted them could not

Page 181.

be collected till the Spring ; nor credit therby given to the K[ing], the affections of his subiects being beyond all grants. he added likewise the afflictions of the time, the interruption of the trade, London being shutt vp the decay & povertie of the commons, vpon wch he cited some examples of foretimes, in pressing their abilities too farr, as 4 R[ichard] 2. &. 3. H[enry] 7. when rebellions did attend it. & 14 H[enry] 8, when the northerne collectors were all slaine, & soe fearfull an apprehension rais'd it'h State, as to satiffie the people, the K[ing] disclaim'd the fact, tranflating it to his counsellors. the counfellors from themselves did impute it to the Judges, the Judges to the Cardinall, w^{cb} shewes the danger they were in, & what effects may follow too great a load & pressure. all w^{ch}

Page 182.   he said were/ reasons against giving at that time. & soe alfo he retorted that common argument of necsesitie against the supplie of that necessitie soe pretended, vsing therin the diftinction given by Bracton, of the three sorts & orders of necessitie, *affectata, invincibilis*, & *improvida*. of wch he thought the necessitie that was argued, to be neither affected nor invincible ; but improvident & voluntarie, wch could be noe incouragment to giving, when those that had spent the former, must be mafters of that store & soe their supplie should be but the ruine of themselves. ffor other means of subsistence for the [King] the second part of the division wch he made, he laid this groundworke & position, that subsidies were not proper for the ordinarie expenc & charge, but the provision was for that in the ordinarie income & revenew. that *Com-*

mune periculum, commune trahit auxilium, common support & aid should be for common dangers. Lands and reveneues were the proper store of princes. that soe was the inftitution of their goverment, soe had beene the practise in foretimes. & three things he said were requisit to a K[ing] & for those ther must be a conftant abilitie in the State. the first, to defend him self against the/ invasions of his enemies, the second to ayd his confederats & allies, the third to reward the merits of his servants, of wch what wanted at that time, was wanting to the K[ing]. wch being ther confest needed noe arguments to prove it, but a reparation in that pointe, was that worke wch would commend them. ffor this, he said, he would first search the causes, & then propound some remedies, as his reason should suggest them.

Page 183.

of the causes, in the first place he ranckt the fraud of officers & servants, inftancing the Cuftomes, of whom one ffarmer, by a medium of seven years, was knowne to gett 50000^{li} p annum. the second was the Spanish League & treatie, wherin was lost & spent more then arithmaticke could accompt, wheras from them they had alwaies gott by warr. the third, the erecting of new offices wth large ffees & the continuanc of some others that were vnnecessarie & vnprofitable ; as the Presidentship of yorke & wales, wch were a great burden to the K[ing] & noe less oppression to the subiect, the like wherof was intended for the west & by an order of Councell soe resolvd 31 H[enry] 8, but declin'd by the wisdome of that/ Countrie, wch would rest vpon the Common Law of England. fowrthlie,

Page 184.

multiplicitie of offices in one man, who could not serve them faithfullie, & by that means hindred others from preferment, whose reward, if they merited, must come from the revenewes of the Crowne, such places being possest. fiftlie, the diforders of the houshould, through the abuse of ministers, who from a shop leapt presentlie to the greencloth ; for inftances therin naming Cranfeild & Harvie. fixtlie, excess of pensions & annuities, of wch he said, the state had then more charge then the whole goverment had borne from the Conquest to that time : & that they grew into a perpetuitie & continuanc by being bought & sould, as if ther were erected a new market for such wares. seventhly, portage for monie, ther being allowd twelve penc a pound out of the revenewes that were gather'd, wheras that service might be done wthout the least deduction. eightlie, the grant of ffee farms, & privie seales, wheras guifts & rewards should confift of offices & honors, not of the treasures or inher[it]anc of the Crowne. these he alledg'd, were amongst others, the causes of that want, from whenc he did defcend/ to the consideration of the remedies. those he distinguisht into two, removent & promovent, as phisitians vse in medicines. for the removent, he propounded the contraries to those causes, ye frauds to be corrected, treaties to be left, vnnecessarie offices retrench't, (citing for that the presidents 19 H[enry] 7. & 22 H[enry] 8. when the like was done), multiplicitie of offices to be broken, abufes of the houshould to be rectified by the ould formes & inftitutions, graunts & annuities resum'd, the sheriffs in each countie to bring in the revenews to the exchequer, & largess to be spar'd till the treasures did abound, as was provided by the ftatute 9 H[enry] 4. that noe man should begg, till the K[ing] were out of debt, whenc that clause in patents (by a speciall provision on the pointe) *ex mero motu*, did come in. thefe for the removents he propounded. ffor the promovent, he added three perticulars. firft the inclosing of waste grounds, wherby ther might be a large augmentation to the Crowne, wth an increase & benefitt to the Kingdome, the K[ing] having 31 forrests, besides parks, wch contayne a mass of lands, that then yeelded nothing but a charge. secondlie, the goverment of Ireland to be rectified/ wch he said antientlie did bring in 30000^{li} a year in the daies of E[dward] 3. when silver was but a five groats an ounce, notwthstanding the increase therin, it then beinge worse then nothing. thirdlie, the king's rents to be improv'd, w^{ch}, he alledg'd, would bear a third part of increase, & that would be a good addition to the ordinarie of revenew, wch ought to bear the ordinarie of expence. that soe 6 E[dward] 3. that king did vndertake it, soe 50 E[dward] 3. 6 R[ichard] 2. 5 H[enry] 4. 1 H[enry] 5. 11 H[enry] 6. 1 E[dward] 4. 1 H[enry] 7. 11 H[enry] 8. it was both declar'd & ordained. & that in the roll 27 E[dward] 3. n° 9, it was said, that the K[ing] in fowrteene years warr wth ffrance did not once charge his subiects because he had good officers. vpon all wch he concluded wth a desire to sitt, & mov'd for a committee to set downe those or such other heads as should be thought helpfull to that service, wch would give the beft aid & sub-

Page 186.

fiftenc to the K[ing]. that soe they might be represented to his ma^tie wth a desire for time to treat & handle them according to the importance of the worke. he had by the waie vpon the point of improvidenc obferv'd some diforders in the Admiraltie. the navie he said wch was the charge of the Lo[rd] Admirall had not in/ the daies of Q[ueen] El[izabeth] danc't a pavine, lying vpon the water, soe long time in readiness w^thout action, that that great place was not committed in ould time to the trust of soe great persons: great persons had enioyd places of great title, but by the wisdome of the elders, men of sufficiencie & meritt were onlie appointed to such offices.

that tradesmen were mafters of the ordinanc till 20 H[enry] 8. & after the nobilitie once possest it, it had never beene well executed. that the Admiraltie in the raigne of E[dward] 3. was divided into the South & North, as being in the iudgment of that prince toomuch for one command, though then it seem'd both that & manie others were too little. to wch notes & arguments made by him, others by others were then added, as their fancies or memories did suggest them. that ther was noe ingagment, as 'twas vrgd. that ther was noe power to ingage the kingdome but by Act. that if ther had beene an ingagment it was quitt, the last parliament having given fower hundred thoufand pounds towards it, besides the subsidies then granted, & yet noe warr proclaim'd, noe enemy diclar'd. naie further by induction it was argued that ther/ was noe necessitie, & that drawne from the forme of preparation. for, it was said, that the land souldiers were all prest

& at their Rendezvous in May, the marriners in April, the Victuall & provisions shipt in March, wherof fower months store was spent wthout moving from the harbors, & the men soe long vnder paie and entertainment, to a vast expenc & charge wth out anie service to the K[ing], wch was not covenable wth the necessitie then pretended, more being monthlie wasted then at that time was requir'd. to all w^{ch}, except that last, the King's Sollicitor gave an answear, but that he baulkt, for to denie the argument he could not, the inferenc being soe cleer, that such vnnecessarie preparations & expences prov'd rather an excess then a necessitj. to denie the perticulars that made vp the induction he dar'd not, their truth being knowne to all men. to grant both the induction & the inferenc, & in the fact denie it, was as dangerous as absurd, it supposing a necessitie wth out reason, & an improvidenc more shamefull then the wante. this therfore he declin'd, but to the rest replied, making first a proteftation for himself, that having two capacities, one as a member of that house, theother as a servant to the K[ing] he would wth out/ partialitie express himself, not houlding of Cephas or Apollo[s] but to the reason of the case, & in the integritie of his conscienc, as his iudgment & opinion should direct him. ffor the ingagment, he held that reallie they were bound, the dissolution of the treaties being the effect of the declaration of the parliament, & the warr intended caus'd by the dissolution of the treaties, for wch the grant last made was not a fatiffaction but an erneft, the obligation houlding to the occasfion not to the time.

for the not knowing of the enemie, he said, it was but

want of ceremonie to the act, &, at moſt but a dispensation for the present, not a dissolution of the bond, wherin he wish't they should be suitors to the K[ing] to remove that scruple of their ielosie. ffor the houlding of places by men of noe experienc (acknowledging the person that was meant, & his relations to him) he desir'd it might not be a preiudice to the publicke if he had beene in fault; but that precedenc might be given to the meritt of the cause & the generall first preferd, that perticular comming after. ffor the afflictions of the time, he said, those were the powers of god, & could not be prevented, nor would they excuse their not resistance of their/ enemies. their enemies, he said, were arm'd, & if they satt still, theothers would not be idle, but either in Ireland or elswher make some attempt vpon them, wch would putt them to more trouble & more charge then then was sought for. & some having obiected the season of the year, that the time was past for the ffleet to putt to sea, & that the King's estate at home was like a leaking ship, not [to] be ventur'd further vntill it were carin'd, he anſweard that the designe was secret, & therfore that the reason was not knowne. & if a leaking ship were set vpon by enemyes, that all the marriners must not looke to the stopping of the leake & let the ship be taken, the greater danger first must be oppos't & look't to: outward attempts are violent, inward difeases bear delay, therfore he concurrd wth the opinion of the Councellors that it was fitt to give, & that onlie to be the businefs of that time, but for the *quantum* he refer'd it to the house.

this was followd by some others of that kinde, & oppos'd againe by manie of the contrarie. the ingagment was still prest, as the maine argument of the Court, & one infer'd from thenc, that part of the Pallatinat was propounded to be restord/ vpon the treatie, & K[ing] J[ames] did then refuse it, changing the resolution of his course ; soe as if the ingagment were retrencht, the warr intended must be left, & soe the Palsgrave should have preiudice by their means, wch would breed a couldness in their frinds, a confidenc in their enemies, the one by an opinion of vnwillingness, the other of disabilitie in the kingdome. this had as small authoritie as beleife, it comming from a gentleman that was seldome fortunat in that place. he was a servant to the Palsgrave, fecretarie to his Q[ueen] & one that had a faire education, & some hope, in his yonger daies of studie; but in his exercise & practise, art had confounded nature, or time both, that mostlie his affections had preiudice by his reasons. that partie restitution, wch he spake of, noe man did credit or beleive, noe such effects to be emergent from those treaties, wch toomuch had beene tried. the point of the ingagment was againe answear'd, not onlie from the fact but from the intention of the house, wherin it was remembred that soe carefull they had beene to avoid that rocke & shelf, as both in the declaration, wch preceded, & in the preamble of the Act, that was/ made an explanation of the former, all words & sillables were stroke out that might carrie an interpretation to that sence.

much time & labor being spent in those arguments & disputes, & manie more intending still to speake, the house perceav'd the resolution was not neer, & therfore left the further agitation for that time (the daie being farr o'respent) setling it by an order to be resum'd againe the morrow. all men difcernd that the violenc would be great. the Courtiers, being fearfull, grew exasperated for their frinds, whom they sawe aym'd & pointed at, & did doubt some neerer touch. the others likewise, by the opposition made more quicke, in opening their greivances finding still more greivance. their owne motions warm'd them, & their affections were inflam'd by reflection on themselves. the danger of the kingdome, their owne perticular dangers, hasarded for the pleasure of one man, rais'd their apprehension on thefe iniuries, & their resolutions to requite them. the newtralls were not manie that had exemption from those passions & shar'd not in that contestation of affections. some ther were, whom fear, & ignoranc divided, that stood in expectation of the issue, & wthout reference to the cause/ resolvd to be the victors. but those were few & not considerable in the question. the truth of what was vrg'd being most obvious & apparant, those whom noe privat interests did move, were bent wholie to complaint; those whom the Court posseft were as ernest to decline it. either part in the remainder of that daie labord the strengthening of their side. infinit was the practise vs'd wth all men, to sound & gaine them, wherin the Courtiers did exceed. noe promises or perswasions were toomuch to make one profelite in that faith. whom ambition had made corruptible, their offerings did allure, &, what reason could not, hope did then effect.

this being the preparation of that night, the worke next

daie beganne wth a remembrance of ye pardon to the Jesuit, & a calling for the petition in that pointe; w^ch, though it seem'd an act of aggravation to the Courtiers, was seconded by another mention of that kinde, that had noe relation to that worke, but then came accidentalie from the Countrie, certified as an occurrence of the time, wch wrought soe powerfullie on the house, as did foment their ielosie, increasing/ the difficultie of atonement, & making the conteftation farr more strong. the perticular was this, some Justices of the peace in Dorfetshire having vpon suspition or intelligenc, search't a papist's house & ther found an altar, copes, crucifixes, books, relicks, and other popish stuffe, & thervpon committed the owner of the house for refusing to take the oaths according to the Lawe, a Letter was sent them from the Court, sign'd by the Secretarie of State, requiring them forthw^th to redeliver the stuffe, wch they had taken away, & to sett at libertie the partie. this by those iuftices was certified to their frinds, they, as they thought it necessarie, did represent it to the house, w^ch, taking it in to the number of their greivances, though they did not much dispute it, did much revolve it in the confideration of their thoughts, that at that time, such countenanc should be given to soe great offendors of the Law, that the Law must be control'd in the favor of such persons, & the ministers of Justice, who were faithfull in their offices, receave an increpation for their duties (for soe the letter did implie), & that/ wher religion was involv'd, this also went as an ingredient of the time into the matter & composition of diftast. though the formall deliberation

Page 194.

Page 195.

were refer'd to the Committee that was appointed for the pardon, in point of remedie & redress, yet the evill was then resented, and the cause not doubted to be knowne, wch gave it an influenc into the agitations of that time. wherin five things were first propounded to be presented to the K[ing] for religion, to make a countermine in that against the bouldness & practise of the adversaries, wthout wch ther could be noe more expected from their enterprises, then there happened to the Israelits while the accursed thing was wth them; & for this to have the king's answear that was spoken of vpon their generall petition therin made, to be rendred in full parliament, that it might be recorded in both houses to receave the qualitie of a lawe. secondlie, that if ther were a reall purpose for a warr, the enemy might be knowne, & some publicke diclaration to that end. thirdlie, that a grave Counsell might be setled, to rectifie the disorder of affaires. ffowrthlie,/ that the king's revenew might be lookt into to stop the leaks in that, & to restore it to its naturall strength & fulness, wthout wch they could not be wthout povertie in the crowne, greivanc & oppression in the goverment. Lastlie, that the doubt of impositions might be cleer'd & an answear in that pointe, wthout wch noe man could saie what trulie was his owne, & soe not know how to promise or to give. & to prove the demands soe parliamentarie & noe capitulation wth the K[ing] the president 22 E[dward] 3. was vouch't, when like petitions were exhibited vpon less reasons from that house. the necessitie therof was likewise prest from the consideration of the kingdome, wch was said to be soe

Page 196.

weake that w{th}out some help therin, it could neither supplie the K[ing] nor yet support it self. Some things were said in answear vnto those, & some passages of the former daie were mention'd wth some asperitie & sharpness, wherin one Clarke went on soe farr in favor of the D[uke] cenforiouslie to tax the exceptions to the Admirall, as in his speach he term'd them bitter invectives. at wch being interrupted by a generall exclamation of the house, to preserve/ their wonted gravitie & ye dignitie of their members, he was cried vnto the barr. vpon this he was w{th}drawne for the consideration of his punishment, that had not more expressions then new waies.

manie delivered their opinions, & most different. Some to have him excluded from that house, others forever to debarr him. some likewise did propound an imprisonment, & mulct, & wth varietie in those, both for the place, and summe. others, more favorable, mov'd onlie for an acknowledgment of his fault, & that also wth some differenc; some would have had it acted at the barr, others but in his place, & ther wanted not that would have wholie had him pardon'd, &, perhaps, that scarcelie thought him faultie: but the receav'd opinion was that wch divided betweene these; not to make the severitie too great least it might relishe of some spleene, nor yet by lenitie to impeach the iustice of the house, but that the example might secure them from the like presumption in the future; therfore his censure was, to be committed to the Sariant, & ther to stand a prisoner during the pleasure of the house.

this being soe resolv'd on, the delinquent was cal'd

52   NEGOTIUM POSTERORUM.

Page 198. in,/ who kneeling at the barr had that sentence ther pronounc't, & soe the Sariant did receave him. this iudgment, as their whole proceeding in like cases, is observable for their order. their gravitie is great in all things, this more punctiallie does express it. for to avoid confusion & disturbanc on noe occasion, at noe time, is it lawfull for a man in one daie to speake to one business above once, though his opinion altered, though his reason should be chang'd, more then in suffrage wth the generall vote at last, when the question is resolv'd by a single yea, or noe. noe personall touches are admitted in anie argument or dispute, noe cavills or exceptions, nor anie member to be nam'd ; or wher ther is contrarietie & dissent may ther be mention of the persons but by periphrasis & discription. all bitterness is excluded from their dialect, all words of scandall & aspersion; noe man may be interrupted in his speech, but for transgression of that rule, or breach of some other order of the house (as for the intermixing of their business, when one matter is on foote, to stirr another before the decision
Page 199. of the former, wch in noe case is allowable) in all/ other things, the priviledg houlds throughout ; the business, as the person, has that freedome to pass quietlie to the end; noe disparitie or odds makes a differenc in that course ; he that does first stand vp, has the first libertie to be heard; the meanest burgess, has asmuch favor as the best knight or counsellor, all sitting in one capacitie of Commoners, & in the like relation to their Countries.

if two rise vp at once the Speaker does determine it ; he that his eye sawe first ha's the precedence given, soe as noe distaste or exception can be taken either for the order, or the speach. I note this the more perticularlie by the way, for the honor of that house. noe wher more gravitie can be found then is represented in that Senat. noe court ha's more civilitie in it self, nor a face of more dignitie towards strangers. noe wher more equall iustice can be found, nor yet, perhaps, more wisdome; but that is out of the consideration of this case, wch I observ'd onlie for the gravitie of the house, against wch that violation being made, that censure did attend it, the debate wherof prevented the greater worke in hand wch for that cause & interruption was defer'd./ that gentleman being in some neerness to the D[uke] this made him reflect more sensiblie on himself, & by his neighbours fire to thinke his house in danger. all his adherents tould him it was an approach vpon his saftie. the advise he had was much to indeavor an accommodation wth the parliament. the errors most insisted on, were said, to be excusable, if retracted; that the disorders of the Navie might be imputed to the officers, that the wante of Counsell might be satiffied by a free admission to the Board. the greatest difficultie was conceav'd to rest in religion, & the ffleet. for the first, the ielosie being deriv'd from his protection given to Mountague; for the latter, that it had soe vnnecessarie a preparation & expence : & yett in both, that ther might be a reconciliation for himself. Sending the ffleet to sea, & giving others the Command was propounded as a remedie for the one; having these reasons to support it, that the designe could not be knowne; nor, if ther wanted one, that iudg'd by

Page 200.

the success; & the success was answerable but by those that had the Action. for the other, it was said, that the leaving of Mountague/ to his punishment, & the wthdrawing that protection would be a satiffaction for the present, wth some publicke declaration in the pointe, & a faire parting of that meeting : that the danger of the time was a great cause of the dislike; that the dislike had vsher'd in most of those questions that were rais'd, therfore to free them from that danger, would dissolve the present difficulties & facilitat the waie to a future temper for agreement. that noe deniall could be look't for in the resolutions of the parliament, nor counsells for their help, such suspitions being rais'd. the ffleet must needs goe foorth to color the preparation, & the returne might yeeld something to iustifie the worke, at least in excuse & apologie for himself, by tranflation of the fault. these & the like counfells were presented to the D[uke] wch wrought an inclination for the inftant that gave his frinds some hope: but those that were about him gave it an alteration in the cabanet, soe vnhappie are great persons to be obnoxious to ill councells, & some by everie aer of flatterie to be moveable,/ not having constancie in themselves: of wch this D[uke] was a full character & instance, who, being vncertaine to his councells, provd vnfaithfull to himself. he had once determin'd to be guided by his frinds, but his parasits were more powerfull to distract him from their principles, wch then increas'd his troubles, & after prov'd his ruine. yet something was chang'd of the forme of former purposes. he then resolv'd that the ffleet should be sent forth, & presentlie design'd another generall to command it; in the west he was perswaded to make triall of some arts, & by some overtures from himself to remove the harbord ielosie; soe ignorant are such parasits in the knowledg of great Councells, as what in their weake iudgments does seeme probable, they thinke feafable wth others, not weighing the manie eyes of Argus that peirce through their light cobwebs, but, like to conies having scarce shadow for their ears yet taking all their bodies to be cover'd; soe is their whole time vers't in the corrupt sceane of flatterie, that in the end the[y] act it on themselves. according to that wisdome 'twas resolv'd on, that the D[uke] should shoot in person/ some new arrowes. to wch end was prepar'd (for all things were readie at his becke) the king's answear to the petition for religion, & this to be presented by his hands, as the influenc of his labors, robbing his mafter both of the honor & the worke. to this purpose, the next morninge a message was pretended from the K[ing] for a meeting of both houses. the occasion intimated was some generall diclarations from his Matie, wch being to be deliver'd by the D[uke] the Lo. Tresurer, the Lo. Conway, & Sr John Coke, it was desir'd both of the Lords & Commons, respectivlie in their places, that their members might have licence for that service, the former exception having beene an inftruction on that pointe. the place appointed was chrift church hall, wch being accepted & leaue given as was desir'd, all other things were left & everie man addreft him to the place. Some doubt ther was for forme vpon

Page 203.

the message to the Commons, it making mention of both houses, & in that case the Speaker must have gone, & his mace beene borne before him, but if it intended the Committees of the houses, then that ceremonie to be left, wherin a short entercourse being made for ex-/planation in the pointe, & it being resolvd that the Committees onlie were intended, in that forme they went to the expectation of the worke.

The Lo. Keeper made the entrance; that wheras formerlie to the petition for religion his ma^{tie} had given a gratious answear in the generall, & promis'd likewise to make it more perticular, he had then accordinglie perform'd it to the fatiffaction of their harts, article by article refolving it, & that in the antient waie of parliaments to be recorded in both houses, wch was to be delivered by the D[uke], who besides had some other things of speciall importanc in his charge to expedit the business in hand, wch were to be propounded from his ma^{tie}. this, he said, he was by the King's command to intimat, wch some beleevd & noe man doubted of the meaninge. that the overture should be his, & the act appropriat to the D[uke]. all men did see it ftudied but a redintegration for the other, & had respect to that wch was to follow from his mouth, as a fomentation to an oyntment; or like to pills that have some sweetness ouer them to make their reception the/ more eafie. but that prologue being past, the D[uke] then entred wth his part, wch thus wth more hope then satiffaction he deliver'd.

My Lords & gentlemen, his Matie hath this daie

laid soe great a charge vpon me, that looking vpon myne owne weakness, I apprehend the weight of it, but when I confider that it is fitt for a K[ing] to deale plainlie wth his people, in that respect it fall's fitlie on me that have neither rhetoricke nor art.

In two words I could give y^u an answear, that all y^r desires are granted; but it wilbe fitter for y^r satiffaction to hear the perticulars read of the petition y^u exhibited & then the answears to them.

vpon this, the petition & answear were both read, the first of wch as we have formerlie inserted, according to the proprietie of its place, we will heer also add the other, that aswell their truth & substanc may be seene, as the vse & application to that worke, wch having some obliquitie, detracted from the expectation of the thing, the effects wherof will heerafter be observable. onlie/ the answear has relation to this place, wch thus was represented to the severall remedies propos'd.

Page 206.

to the 1. this is well allowed of, & for the better performanc of what is desir'd, letters shalbe written to the two Archbishops, & from them letters to goe to all the ordinaries in their severall provinces to see this done & the severall ordinaries to give accompt of their doings heerin to the Archbishops respectivelie, and they to give accompt to his Matie of their proceedings heerin.

to the 2. this is approved by his ma^{tie} & the chancelor of each Vniversitie shalbe required to cause due execution of it.

to the 3.   that his ma^{tie} likes it well, soe as it be applied onlie to such ministers as are peaceable, orderlie, & conformable to the church-Goverment. ffor pluralities, non-residence, & commenda's, theise are now moderated, & the Archbishop affirmes ther be now noe dispensations for pluralities granted. & for avoyding nonresidence the Cañon in that case provided shalbe dulie/ put in execution. for Commenda's they shalbe but sparinglie granted onlie in cases wher the exilitie & smalness of the Bishopricke requires it. Also his ma^{tie} will cause that the benefices belonging to him shalbe well bestowed. & for the better propogating of religion his ma^{tie} recommends to the house of parliament that care may be taken & provision made, that everie parish shall allowe competent mayntenanc for an able minister. & that the owners of parsonages impropriat would allowe to the Vicars, Curats & ministers in villages & places belonging to their parsonages sufficient stipends & allowances for preaching ministers.

to the 4.   the lawe in this case shalbe put in execution. & further ther shalbe letters written to the Lo. Tresurer, & also to the Lo. Admirall, that all the ports of the realme & the creekes

& members therof be straightlie kept, & strick't searches made to this end, & proclamation shalbe to/ recall both the children of noblemen, & the children of anie other men, & they to returne by a day. Also the maintenance of Seminaries or Schollers ther, shalbe punished according to Lawe.

to the 5. if his Matie should finde or be informed of anie concourse of recusants to the Court, the Lawe shalbe stricktlie followed, & his ma^{tie} is pleased that by a proclamation the Brittishe & Irishe subiects shalbe put in the same case. &, as his ma^{tie} hath provided in the treatie wth ffrance, soe his purpose is to keep it, that none of his subiects shalbe admitted into his service or the service of his roiall consort the Q[ueen] that are popish recusants.

to the 6. the Lawe in this case provided shalbe put in execution, & a proclamation shalbe to the effect desired; & that noe man that is iustlie suspected of poperie shalbe suffered to be keeper of anie of his ma^{ties} prisons.

to the 7. this is fit to be ordered accordinglie as it is/ praied, & it shalbe soe published by proclamation.

to the 8. the K[ing] will give order to his learned councell to consider of the grants, & will doe accordinglie as is desired.

to the 9. his Matie leaves the lawes to their owne

	course, / & will giue order in the pointe of excommunication as is desired.
to the 10.	this his Matie thought fit, & will giue order for it.
to the 11.	the lawes & acts of State in this case provided shalbe followed & put in execution.
to the 12.	for this the lawes in force shalbe forthw^th executed.
to the 13.	the K[ing] gives assent heervnto, & will see that observed heerin wch hath beene commanded by him.
to the 14.	this shalbe done as is desir'd.
to the 15.	it is fit this statute be executed, & the penaltie shall not be dispensed w^th.
to the 16.	his ma^ties cares are & shalbe extended ouer that kingdome of Ireland, & he will doe all/ that a religious K[ing] should doe for reftoring & establishing of true religion ther.

these answears being read the D[uke] went on as followeth.

his Matie hath taken well y^r putting him in mynde of these things, & if y^u had not prest it, he would have done it of himselfe. he doth not this to draw y^u on; but what he hath done is to discharge his concienc & the dutie of a sonne to his ffather, who commanded him, as by his will, in his death bed, to shew to the world assoone as he was married, that he did not marrie the religion but the person of his Ladie.

this I am commanded by his Matie to deliver in that pointe.

I am now to give y^u an accompt of the ffleet & the preparation that has beene.

the first time & last I had the honor & happiness to speake before y^u, was, in the same business. I call it honor & happiness, because vpon that wch I said then were grounded the councells & resolutions that have made soe marvelous a change/ in all the affaires of chriftendome. & that was soe happie vnto me that I had the honor to be applauded by y^u. now having the same hart to speake w^th, & the same cause to speake in, before the same persons, I doubt not, but I have the same success & approbation.

if y^u looke vpon the change of affaires as they are now, from the time that was then y^u will thinke it little less then a miracle. for at that time the K[ing] of Spaine went conquering on, & was sought to by all the world. he mast'red Germanie, the Pallatinat, & the Valtolinc. the princes of Germanie were weake; & not able to refift & by a treatie he kept all other princes in awe. wheras now the Valtoline is at libertie, the warr is in Italie, the K[ing] of Denmarke hath an armie of 17000 foote, & 6000 horse, & Commissions out to make them 30000. the K[ing]

NEGOTIUM POSTERORUM.

Page 212.

of Swedén diclares himself, the princes of the vnion take hart, the K[ing] of ffrance is ingag'd in a warr against the K[ing] of / Spaine, hath peace wth his subiects, & is ioyned in a league wth Savoy & Venice. this being the state of things then & now, I hope to have from y^u the same success of being well construede, wch then I had : for since that time I have not had a thought, nor entred into an action, but what might tend to the advancement of the business, & please y^r desires. but if I should give eare & credit (wch I doe not) to rumors, then I might speake wth some confusion, fearing not to hould soe good a place in y^r opinion, as then y^u gave me, wherof I shall still have the same ambition & hope to deserve it. when I consider the integritie of myne owne sowle & hart to the K[ing] & State, I receave courage and confidenc, whervpon I make this request, that y^u will beleeve, that if anie amongst y^u in discharge of their opinions & conciences say anie thing that may reflect vpon perticular persons, that I shalbe the last in the world to make application of it to my self, being soe

Page 213.

well assured of y^r iustice,/ that wthout cause y^u will not fall on him that soe latelie was approved by y^u, & who neuer will doe anie thing to irritat anie man to have other opinion of me, then of a faithfull true harted Englishman. & bicause in a continued speech, I cannot give y^u soe good satiffaction in the openinge of this business, therfore I will take this order to make propositions & questions to my self, & answear them aswell as I can. I will beginne wth the time when the resolution was taken for breach of the treaties & allianc, & give this accompt of myne owne actions.

1. quest.   the first question I put to myself, is, by what councells this great enterprise hath beene vndertaken & pursued hitherto.

ans.   .I answear by the Parliament, & desire the diclaration may be read that was made 23° marcij 1623 (wch being done accordinglie by the Atturnie generall, he thus proceeded)

heer my Lords & gentlemen y^u see vpon councell my Master entred into this busine{s when y^u had given the councell & the means/ to execute it. the next part was to sett on worke, that wch was then proposd, the defenc of England, the securitie of Ireland, the assifting his ma^{ties} frinds & allies, the fetting forth of a roiall Navie, of wch the first three were forth-wth vndertaken. & when my master had come to execute thus much, he looked into his purse & found himself vnable for the Navie. yet looking vpon the affaires of chriftendome, found it to be most necessarie. but that is not all.

if he should then have nam'd an enemye & diclar'd a warr, all his marchants goods in Spaine had beene embargued wch are since drawne home, the enemie had beene prepar'd, his frinds not readie to assift the Allianc, not soe easilie drawne in, & soe long a time betweene the diclaration & the action, as would have made the world beleeve he intended nothing.

vpon this his ma^{tie} of famous memorie being at newmarket, wrote to me a letter to London to this effect, that looking into the affaires of chriftendome he thought fitt/ to haue a roiall ffleet set foorth; but wthall he wrote, I have noe monie in my purse but I would have y^u ingage y^r self, y^r owne estate & y^r frinds to sett it forwards. by this means I shall seeme less ingag'd, & other princes, in hope to draw me on, will the sooner come in themselves. heervpon [I] went to it wth alacritie, & knowing that all I have I had from him, I could doe noe less, & held it a happiness that I could once say to the K[ing] S^r y^u may [have] all that y^u gaue floating in y^r service. then I confer'd wth the Councell of warr, the Lo. Conway, Lo. Grandison, Lo. Chichester, Lo. Carew, Lo. Brooke, Lo. Harvie, Sr Robert Mansell, & Sr John Coke & Captaine Low were then present. we first talked of the warr, & then of the means. I neuer spake almost of the business but wth them. I never came to London but I mett wth them, I went to them, or they did me the honor to come to me. I never thought of alteration, nor resolv'd of anie thing but in their companie. when I saw all the materialls readie, ships, ordinanc,/ victuall, all prepar'd, then for the proportions, & the times & levies, it was thought fit to communicat this to the Lords of the Councell, bicause the levies could not be but by them. whervpon I addrest my self to his Matie & praied him to refer it to the Lords. I made the accompt to them wth wch they were all satiffied, & said that if this were put in execution it would doe well. & they were pleas'd to give some attributes to it. about this time his ma^tie sent me into ffrance. I intreated his ma^tie to have a care of the business, that it might be follow'd according to the direction agreed vpon at the Councell table, & the Lo. Tresurer, Lo. Chamberlaine, Lo. Conway, Lo. Brooke were named Committees to see it perform'd.

 this I thought fit to tell y^u that I might shew y^u what great councell this bufiness was carried w^th, & I haue not made anie other step in it, then what I hav[e] tould y^u./

2. quest. the second question, is whither those expences computed for this business at 400000^li. wherof 300000^li. is alreadie disburst. 40000^li.

Page 216.

Page 217.

	more presentlie to be paid & 60000^{li} at the returne of the ffleet, have beene bestowed in that frugall manner as is fit or noe.
ans.	I answear all was manag'd by the proper officers. I laid out monie of myne owne & borrowed of my frinds; but I made it to runne the proper waie, as if it had come out of the Exchequer (to wch Sr John Coke ecchoed, that 44000^{li} his grace had disburst of his owne & 50000^{li} more he had borrowed of a frinde).
3. quest.	whither yet ther be a considerable summe wanting to set out the ffleet, wthout wch it cannot goe to Sea, & whither this ffleet was ever intended to goe foorth or noe.
ans.	I answear to set out this ffleet 40000^{li} is wanting. my master hath anticipated all his revenews, pawnd his lands, & would have pawnd his plate if it would have/ beene accepted; soe that his Matie must lie in miserie vnless some course be taken for his supplie. & for the second part whither it were intended the ffleet should goe forth or noe, I know not what pollicie my master should have to set out a ffleet wth the charge of 400000^{li}. to amuse the world, & lessen his people, & to putt y^u to much hasard. what should my master gaine? would he doe an act never to meet wth y^u againe? certainlie he would never have imploied

Page 218.

soe great a summe of monie, but that he sawe
the necessitie of the affaires of christendome
require it. & it was done wth an intention
to sett it out wth all the speed that might
bee.

4. quest. why was not this wante of monie foreseene
in the first proiect of this whole service, but
comes to be thought vpon soe vnexpected
& dangerouslie, considering the business; at
least why not before the last adiornment,
wherby this meeting is drawne at soe vnseasonable a time.

ans. I answear, this was foreseene, but inter-
rupted/ by vnfortunat accidents; as the death of Page 219.
my gratious master of famous memorie; then
the funerall wch for decencie could not be more
hastned; then the iorney into ffrance & the marriage, wch made more delaies then were expected yet necessarie. Since the parliament
was cal'd y^u haue heard his Maties declaration
that ther was no more time for Councells but
for resolution. & when his ma^tie vnderstood
how lovinglie y^u had given those two subsidies,
he conceav'd they had beene onlie as a present
for his welcome to the Crowne, & did resolve
when they should be presented vnto him, as
he thought the manner was, at the same time
to relate the business more at large, as afterwards he did by Sr John Coke.

5. queſt.   who gave that councell to meet againe when the sickness was soe dangerouslie dispers't.

ans.   I answear, his ma^tie commanded me to tell y^n, the business it self, & the necessitie of that gave that councell. els he [would] not/ have hasarded y^r persons, nor the saftie of the kingdome by dispersing of the plague: if he had beene able to set it forth w^thout y^r help, he would have done it, & trust vpon y^u for supplie afterwards.

but admitt a fault hath beene made, why should the State, the action, the affaires of christendome suffer for it? if it be for my master's honor, wch is now budding, y^r owne good & the kingdomes, why should a perticular man's miſtaking, cause it to miscarie? I hope y^r wisdomes will soe farr peirce through it, as to set it forward.

6. quest.   why should not the king's owne estate help this business?

ans.   Judge whither it hath or noe: seeing y^u gaue soe largelie before, he chose rather to laie out of his owne estate, then to press y^u; & whither ther be not cause to be assured that he will doe more when it shalbe in his power, since he hath alreadie done ſomuch.

7. quest.   but is not the time of the year too farr/ spent for the Navie to goe foorth?

ans.   my Mastere answeard, better the ffleet goe

out & perish half, then now not goe: for it would shew want of Councell & experienc in the designe, wante of courage in the execution, & would argue weakness & beggerie of the kingdome, as not able to goe through wth such a designe. the ends proposd were three, the time yet seasonable for all, wch I would manifest if it were fit to publishe the designes, wch I thinke none of y^u in y^r wisdomes desire to know.

8. quest. whither the eight ships sent to the K[ing] of ffrance, were set out at the charge of the K[ing] or of the subsidie monie, & were to be imploied against the Rochellors.

ans. I answear for the first, it was at the charge of the ffrench K[ing] & for theother it is not at all times fit for kings to give accompt of their councells: but this y^u may know, wch I assure y^u, that they are not, & y^u may iudge of that perticular by the event.

9. quest. y^u will say I was y^r servant to breake the/ Spanish match, but have done as ill in making the ffrench wth worse conditions.

ans. to that I say the contrarie is manifested by the king's answear to y^r petition, wch he hath done wthout breaking anie publicke faith.

10. quest. yea but I serv'd y^u in the breach of the Spanish treatie for perticular spleene & hate of myne owne to Count Olivoro's.

ans.

noe cause had I to hate OLivaro's, who made me more happie then all the world beside: for I had out of his hand papers wch could not otherwise be obtain'd, by wch I gain'd a nation. I am not vindicative, nor wilbe an instrument to doe anie thing by ill means. his intention was to serve his master, but by indirect means. I cann forgive my enemies. I will leaue that business a sleep, wch if it be wakned will prove a lion to devour him that was the author of it. I meane one of myne owne nation who did cooperate wth him.

11. quest.

but hitherto ther ha's beene nothing spoken but of immense charge wch the kingdome/ is not able to bear, if it should continue.

firſt the K[ing] of Denmarke—30000^{li} a month, Manffeilt's armie—20000^{li}. the regiments in the Lowe Countries—8000^{li}. Ireland—2000^{li}. besides twelve ships preparing to second the ffleet.

ans.

ffor this I say make my master cheife of the warr, & by that y^u shall give his allies better assiſtanc then if y^u gaue him—100000^{li}. a month. what is it for his allies to scratch wth the K[ing] of Spaine, to winne a battaile to daie, & to lose one tomorrow, & to get, or lose a towne by snatches. but to goe wth a conquest by land, the K[ing] of Spaine is soe strong it is impossible to doe: but let my master be cheife of the warr & make a diversion by sea, the enemie spends the more, he must draw from other places, & soe y^u give to them. by this kinde of warr y^u send noe coyne out of the kingdome, that wch comes from the subiect is disburst at home, & what cometh out in provisions will returne againe in better commodities, & soe the realme not impoverisht but enrich't.

12. quest. yea but wher is the enemie ?/
ans. make the ffleet readie to goe, my master gave me command to bid y^u name the enemie y^r selves. put the sword into his hands, & he will mayntaine the warr.

make an entrance & afterward it wilbe defraied wth profit. when y^u have diclar'd whom y^u will have for y^r enemie, demand letters of Mart, none shalbe denied; & I have not beene soe idle, but I shall make propositions wher y^r selves may venture to goe & have the honie of the business.

Lastlie my master commands me to praie y^u to have regard of y^r owne healths, & of the season. if y^u lose time y^r monie cannot purchase it. if in this report my weakness hath iniur'd the businefs, the K[ing], the State, the affaires of christendome, I crave pardon for my intentions were good.

after this follow'd the conclusion of the Tresurer, who

72 NEGOTIUM POSTERORUM.

by infinit calculations & accompts was to confound the intelligenc of his hearers. his memorie gave but little, but his papers spake the rest, both wch in this manner he presented.

Page 225. my Lords & gentlemen, I am to make y^u/ a declaration of the king's estate, wch I cannot doe soe perfectlie as I would, being sodenlie cal'd vnto it by the K[ing] in a remote place, wher I wante my books, and manie things are now out of my memorie. what I have to say I will divide into three parts. in the first I will shew in what estate the king's revenew was left by his ffather. secondlie, in what estate his now stands. thirdlie, in what estate he is like to be for the future. vnder the first head, I will diclare his debts. his anticipations. his ingagements.

y^e estate at ffor the firſt, the late K[ing] of famous memorie
y^e death of K. J. was indebted to the citie of London & others, for part of wch the great seale was ingag'd, & for the reſt the bonds of Lords of the Councell wch remayne forfeited, the summe (besides interest) of_____120000^li.

debts. to the wardrobe & other poore men in crying debts at least_____40000^li
to the K[ing] of Denmarke_____75000^li

Page 226. arrears of pensions & other paiments soe great a masse as I will not mention, & lastlie to the/ houshould a good summe but the certaintie I doe not remember.

anticipations. ther was taken vp of his customes and revenewes before hand at least_____50000^li.

NEGOTIUM POSTERORUM. 73

To the Low Countries for the maintenanc of 6000 foote ⸺⸺⸺⸺⸺⸺⸺⸺⸺⸺⸺ *ingagments.*
to Count Manffeilt for the maintenanc of
12000⸺⸺⸺⸺⸺⸺⸺⸺⸺⸺⸺⸺⸺
to rigg, victuall, man, & furnish this great navie, the like wherof England hath not set forth in man's memorie ⸺⸺⸺⸺⸺⸺ ⸺⸺⸺⸺
all wch ingagments were vndertaken aswell for the defenc & saftie of the realme, as for the common cause of religion.

thus was the revenew left; & now for the present state, I am to note two things, his Maties owne debts, & his difbursments.   *ye estate in present*

& heer y^u must remember to his ffather's debts, anticipations, & ingagments, to add these likewife of his owne.

the first when he was prince, wch he borrowed vpon securitie of the Councell for this Navie—20000^{li}. for Count Manffeilt—20000^{li}. & for other publick services somuch as in the/whole is⸺⸺⸺⸺⸺ 70000^{li} *debts as prince.*

Page 227.

the other debt to be added is borrow'd since he was K[ing], of the Citie of London to paie the K[ing] of Denmarke for other services. being ⸺⸺60000^{li}.   *debt since.*

to the K[ing] of Denmarke for entertaynment of— 6000 foote, & 1000 horse, monthly⸺⸺⸺30000^{li}.   *disburfm^{ts}*
for the armes of those companies⸺⸺⸺16000^{li}.
for the fouldiers at Plimouth & Hull⸺16000^{li}.
for the mourning clothes & funeralls⸺12000^{li}.
more to be paid for the mournings &c.⸺16000^{li}.

II.   L

	the charge of the marriage wth the entertaynments & gifts of honor to Ambassadors _____ 40000^{li}.
	to the Q[ueen] for hir expences _____ 5000^{li}.
	to the Q[ueen] of Bohemia for the last half year _____ 10000^{li}.
	to the furnishing of the Navie _____ 300000^{li}.
	more wanting for the navie presentlie _____ 40000^{li}.
	more against the returne _____ 600000^{li}.
y^e estate in expectanc. Page 228. debt.	Now for the third part, wch is the ſtate wherin the K[ing] is like to stand for the future, he remaynes charg'd wth all the ould & new/ debts, & wth full interest for the time before midſomer, & since according to the statute.
anticipation.	he hath anticipated vpon the Cuſtomes & revenew to be due for the year ensuinge. (soe as we are in question how to mayntaine him bred & meat) the summe of _____ 200000^{li}.
ingagm^{ts}	he ſtands ingaged to the K[ing] of Denmarke monthlie for _____ 30000^{li}.
	to Count Manſfeilt monthlie _____ 20000^{li}.
	for the supplie of Ireland monthly _____ 2600^{li}.
	for the regiments in the Low Countries _____ 8500^{li}.
	to the Q[ueen] for her diet yearlie _____ 37000^{li}.
	to the Q[ueen] of Bohemia yearly _____ 20000^{li}.

besides other preparations for defenc of England & Ireland, & for seconding the ffleet.

divers other things being omitted, of wch some were before my time, wherwth I am not acquainted, some since; bicause they are not perfected; nor are the totalls of these caſt vp, bicause the summe in some perticulars are wanting, & I confess my self noe good auditor, & having noe hand to help me, I must desire to be excus'd./

this sceane, thus acted & concluded, the meeting did dissolve. & the report therof, out of their papers, wch were delivered to that end, being made readilie to the houses, amongst the Commons, wher they came onlie to be treated of, some motions presentlie started vp in favor of supplie, thinking those overtures had captiv'd all mens iudgments, & leveld them to the pleasure of the Court. the Tresurer of the King's houshould first beganne drawing his swasorie from the answear in religion. others did follow in like haste to purchase some credit by devotion. amongst whom a lawier, one Mallet did appeer reasoning by presidents against presidents: (for in all the disputes before it being a pinching argument in pointe against the proposition for supplie, that it was vnparliamentarie & vnpresidented in one session to enact seuerall grants of subsidies; therfore he replied) that presidents were at the discretion of all times. that the bill of tonnage & pondage was then limited for a year, wch divers ages past had beene constantlie for life. that that grant likewise wch begann it first for life, was a varying from the elders, that were limitted, & that diverslie from thenc he infer'd the change & alteration of all times, & that the president of one was not the practise of another, therfore in that case alſo, he perswaded, to vse the like libertie as their ffathers. wch I

Page 229.

observe the sooner for the qualitie of the man, that he whose/ profession was the Lawe, & on wch ground he built all the good hopes he had, should argue against presidents, wch are the tables of the Lawe, & soe vnlawlike terme everie act a president, making noe differenc betweene examples & their rules. but the acceptation was according to the worke; &, as that reason was improper for that man, that time was thought improper for that businefs, wch being of great importance, requird greater deliberation & advise, & therfore, those motions being neglected, the debate was then putt off, vpon more mature conceptions to be resum'd next day.

In the meane time those passages were revolv'd that had beene deliver'd at the meeting, & divers were the apprehensions wch did follow them. that the Lo : Keeper, the prime officer of the kingdome should be made subservient to the D[uke] (for soe the act imported, being but an vsher to his businefs) was thought preposterous & inverted. that the king's name must be a servant to his ends, vnder color of some declaration from his Matie, to exhibit an apologie for himself, seem'd as a kinde of wonder. that the whole parliament should be made attendant vpon him, was not wthout a strangenefs, the like/ having seldome beene before. But above all portentous it was thought, that religion should be descended to his vse, & that wch admits noe equall or compeer to troope vp wth the rable of his followers. this was thought much in him soe to assume & take it, but more in those that made that concession to his power. what ever might be promis'd in the words, this

Page 230.

Page 231.

act of deliverie did impeach it, & much of the hope & expectation in that pointe, this forme & circumstanc did obliterat.

besides divers exceptions were emergent, some in the matter, some in the forme of his difcourse. many things of arroganc were observ'd, as in the narrative wch he made of that great change in chriftendome, vsurping that worke vnto himselfe, wch time & providenc had effected, turning fortuities into glorie; those things, or most of them having noe relation to his proiects but in the concurrenc of the time: the ffrench preparations moving on other reasons of their owne that embroild them wth the Spaniar'd : & the Duke of Savoy & Venetian ioyning wth them for their owne interests & safties, whose worke it was & that in contemplation of themselves, by wch the Valtoline was set at libertie./

if the K[ing] of Denmarke did declare, or Sweden, who was then scarcelie heard of (soe envious was time vnto the honor of that person, whom ffortune & virtue had reserv'd for the wonder of the world) yet it was knowne to be in affection to the Palsgrave, though at the instance of his frinds, not induc'd by him, or anie opinion of his meritt, wch mov'd as little wth the other German princes. againe, that expression, wher he spake of Olivaro's, that by him he had gain'd a nation, was soe boafting & thrasonicall, that it seem'd most ridiculous, as if nations, had beene the game & plaie of favorits, who wonne or lost them after their fortunes or their skills. the mention likewise of his owne approbations & applauses, was thought soe neer self flatterie, as it drown'd thé reputation of that truth. besides, manie insolencies were obvious, that had as ill acceptanc, as that in the end of his narration, wher he summ'd vp the whole business of that meeting, pretended to be a diclaration from the K[ing] & he ther calling it an accompt of his owne actions. & that other above all, stating the preparations at his going into ffrance, wher he made, as 'twere, the K[ing]/ his deputie in his absence to [super]intend the progress of that worke. & that perticular in his answear vpon his tenth question & hypothesis intimated for his enemye at home, that he could prove a lyon to devour him, all wch seem'd too insolent & presuming; & that as rash & indifcreet on the fowrth question, wher he rancks the marriage of the Q[ueen] wth those he stiles the vnfortunat accidents of that time. & manie things were iudg'd imperfect in his answears, by wch manie scruples more were rais'd, then that indeavor had resolv'd: but speciallie, in ye point of Councell for that meeting, soe little satiffaction was conceav'd, as the wound became the tenderer for that rubbing, & that search made the orifice more wide. for an aggravation vnto this vpon privat difgusts amongst the Courtiers, the secret was let out of the consultation thervpon, & how the Keeper wth some others, when the proposition for the adiornment was first made, being but the daie before it was, had wth much violenc oppos'd it to the K[ing], wth reasons both of honor & profit to perswade him, & yet were therin master'd by the D[uke], who, like a torrent at resistance, did/ forthwth swell against them, & threatend wth his weight their ruine for that service. this being then diffus'd & credited, as 'twas truth, cast noe small preiudice both on his person & his acts. that also then begann to be fomented by those opposits, who, for the preservation of themselves, studied his subversion. both could not stand togeather, but they must doe or suffer, & the after game is not pleasant in the Court. these therfore did infuse into the humor that was stir'd what gall & vineger they might, & by their privat instruments blowing the coales then kindled, added also more fewell to the fier.

In this state comes the debate to be resum'd, according to the order of the Commons, when to prevent the worst, & ther was reason good to doubt it, a new message was deliver'd from the K[ing], but, being thought an art onlie of diversion for that worke, wanted the effect it look't for, nor was it after in their arguments distinguisht from the former, but both had one ioynt consideration & dispute. the message was brought by Sr Richard Weston Chancelor of the Exchequer, & to this purpose, that the K[ing] taking knowledg of their/ desires to reforme manie things for his service, was well pleas'd in the intention ; but desir'd them to take into consideration that that time was onlie fit for such matters as were of present necessitie & dispatch. that the ffleet staid their resolution, &, though the season were not past, yet it was much spent. that if the plague should fall into the navie, or the armie, the action were lost. that if it should fall amongst themselves it would breed much danger to the kingdome. therfore he desir'd they would presentlie resolue whether vpon those reasons somuch importing his honor they would supplie his necessitie for the setting forth of the ffleet: otherwise that he would take more care for their safties then they themselves, & would doe as he might in such an extremitie. But if they would give him a present dispatch for the supplie, that he promifed in the word of a K[ing] that they should meet againe in winter, & staie togeather till those things might be brought to maturitie, wch were then in conception; & that he would then doe whatsoeuer belongd to a good & gratious K[ing], desiring them to remember that it was his firft request that/ euer he made to them.

Page 236.

this message was seconded, wthout anie interim of consideration first admitted, by a long compos'd oration of the Master of the wards, Sr Robert Nanton, who, in his former times having beene publicke orator for that place, the Vniversitie, thought it his dutie then to render some demonstrations of his skill, but found that the could rhetoricke of the Schools was not that moving eloquenc wch does affect a parliament. his labor was more then his success, &, after much indeavor his worke return'd in vaine. passing a long preamble, he first spake of the manner of the gift, & then made his perswasions for their giving, wch he perchance intended for a figure, others conceav'd to be irregular & preposterous. for the manner he propounded readiness & freeness, qualities as he said, that would be a doubling to the guift, endear the curtesie, heighten the obligation & their thanks, vsing that sentenc for a kindness gott wth difficultie, *satis esse si tali beneficio ignoscas.* for the guift he vrg'd divers topicks to induce it ; the honor of the K[ing], the reputation of the kingdome, defence of their allies, support of the Vnion, preser-/ vation of religion, the safties of his Matie, the nobilitie, & themselves, w^{ch}, he concluded, if they prevail'd not in that case, must be esteem'd a prodigious signe & omen, of some great iudgment neer at hand. this was follow'd by some others who had the same meaning, & like reasons ; & one insifted vpon the expressions of the Admirall, wch the rest forbore to mention, saying that he had prov'd himself then capable of that place, deserving of the rest, being soe well diclar'd a Logitian, a rhetoritian, & a charitable man, wch should abate the ielosies that were had, & therfor they should give. another argued from a supposition of invasion, in wch case all would give, & infer'd thenc, that the contrarie being ment, the reason of contraries should perswade them. fuch was the logicke of the Court. but those sophistries & sophisters, if they were worthy of that name, were not somuch answear'd as confounded by the arguments & obiections on the contrarie. wherin was alledg'd that when formerlie they had given they had hopes & expectations for the Countrie, then ther was nothing but discouragments, pardons to Jesuits, protection given to papists,/ exinanition of the lawes, increpation of good ministers, interruptions of the trade, losses & spoiles by pirats, & though complaints were often made, & means for remedie at hand, yet noe releife was gotten, nor succor could be had. that the present newes from Rochell, wch they had alwaies aided, what ever was pretended, was that

Page 237.

Page 238.

their ships were intended against them, & their owne armes to be turn'd against their frinds. that wheras last they went wth praier & fasting to their Countries, then they might take vp sackcloth & ashes in their iorney. that the greivances were great wch the whole kingdome suffer'd, & if they gave an addition of supplie that would make them greater. these & their like possest the iudgment of the house, against the arguments made for giving. the scope likewise of the message was conceav'd, pressing the· resolution to that straight, but to prevent the considerations of the State, & by a deniall of supplie to color the dissolution of the parliament. this was difcern'd & knowne, & against this the counterworke did trench, to shew the necessities of the kingdome, & the ill councells for that meeting, yet not to denie to give. wherin the first mayne overture that was made came from Sr Robert Philips, who both did answear the/ arguments that were made, & oppos'd them wth new reasons.

the arguments for giving he reduc'd to the heads of honor & necessitie, & for the first, he said, that the honor of a K[ing] stood not in acts of will, but on designes that were grounded by advise, & a constant application of good councells, that what euer did succeed the iudgment & direction might seeme good.

ffor the necessitie, he alledg'd, that it was the common argument in parliaments, & their experienc had inform'd them, that that necessitie had beene formerlie but for the satiffaction of the Courtiers.

that if it were reall then, yet that it was but occasion'd by their means; their luxuries & excesses had wasted first the treasures, & then expos'd the honor of the K[ing]. ffrom thenc he descended to note some presidents of ould times, some of their owne, some out of other nations. at home, he observ'd, in the daies of H[enry] 3. that a supplie demanded was refus'd, vntill ther were a confirmation of their liberties. in the raigne of H[enry] 6. likewise, when the D[uke] of Suffolke did ingross the favor of the K[ing] assum'd the goverment to himself, dispos'd of honors, alien'd the crowne lands, & alone treated a marriage for that K[ing] the like refuse was made, till he that before had had the applause of parliament, then/ receav'd their censure; & when that pointe of reformation was beganne, a supplie did forthw[th] follow it. the like, he said, had beene abroad, & that all times, all States almost, could witness it. that in ffrance when the black prince had taken the ffrench K[ing] prisoner, the estates being then convented, & the Dolphine demanding a releife for redemption of his ffather, the greivances of the people were exhibited, & delaie being made in them, the assiftanc was denied vntill he did complie for the satiffaction of the parliament. that in Spaine likewise, when for the warr against the Moors a parliament was assembled at Toledo, & an ayd demanded for that service, the Conde de Laro did stand vp, & disswaded a contribution in that case till the burdens of the people were releas'd, w[ch] accordinglie was insifted on, & that not held, wth that supercilious state & nation, a breach of faith or dutie. that England was the last Monarchie that yet retain'd hir liberties, let them not perish now, let not posteritie complaine that we have done for them worse then our ffathers did for vs. their presidents are the safest steps we tread in. Let vs not now forsake them, least their fortunes forsake vs. wisdome & councell made them happie, & the like causes will have the like effects. thus spake that gentleman/ & concluded not to denie to give, but to prepare an answear to the K[ing] wth a remonstranc of their reasons for the worke of reformation, moving for a Committee to prepare it, & Sr Robert Mansell, one of the Counsellors of warr, & a member of that house, to be ther commanded to render his knowledg for the action, whither it did proceed by good deliberation & advise, worthie the honor of the State, & such as had beene pretended.

this made a levell to the way, & shew'd the end was aym'd at, wch the Courtiers againe indeavor'd to divert, & to that purpose the chancelor of the Dutchie did replie vpon that wch he thought ye moſt prevailing argument, & having prest his whole faculties to that service, thus in much art delivers them.

Let noe man dispise the presidents of antiquitie; noe man adore them. though they are venerable yet they are noe gods. examples are strong arguments, being proper, but times alter, & wth them, oft, their reasons. everie parliament, as each man, must be wise wth his owne wisdome, not his ffathers. a dramme of present wisdome is more pretious then mountaines of that wch was practis'd/ in ould times. men of good affections have beene knowne to give ill counsells. soe they may now if nothing but examples doe perswade them. if we goe this way I must say, as the children of the prophets, *mors est in olla*.

were all our enemies heer, & had their voice in this assemblie, would they not say, not give? Let vs not therfore be guided by their rules; but, leaving other things of difficultie, yeeld to the king's request, & at this time give, bicause if we give not now, we cannot give againe.

this being soe pressing & patheticall, mov'd more in apprehension then in iudgment. some did conceave a fear from that prophecie wch he made, & from his close, measuring his words by his intelligenc.

but the esteeme of presidents did remayne, wth those that knew the true value of antiquitie; wherof a larger collection was in store to direct the resolution in that case, wch thus contain'd both reason & authoritie.

While those remain'd in the service of K[ing] J[ames] who were bred by Q[ueen] El[izabeth] & traind in the goverment of that time, the crowne/ debts were not great, grants & commissions less complain'd of, trade florish't, pensions more few, & all things of moment carried by publicke councell, that, though ther wanted something of the former, yet ther was much more happiness then at this time. noe honors, noe iudiciall places set to sale, laws executed against preists, papists restrain'd & punish't, their resort to Ambassadors debar'd by his Maties direction to

Page 243.

his minifters & by his penne diclaring his dislike of that profession. noe vast expences then in fruitless embassies & treaties, nor anie tranfcendent power to be master of all business, the Councell table houlding hir antient dignitie. naie soe long as Somersett stood in grace, & had the trust both of the privie seale & signett, he oft would glorie iustlie that ther had past neither to his frinds nor him, anie large grants of lands or pensions from the K[ing]: he induc'd noe monopolies for the greivanc of the people ; nor made a breach vpon nobilitie by exposing honors vnto sale, refusing/ in perticular, that wch has since beene taken, the Lo. Roper's office, for his barronie.

Page 244.

the Match wth Spaine then off'red wth out anie further toleration in religion then Ambassadors were allow'd, vpon discoverie of their falshood was disswaded, & the K[ing] left in such distrust of Gondamar, that he term'd him a iugling Jacke, & Empericke.

thus stood the ftate when his misfortunes clouded him. since wch time wee know the treatie for the marriage was renew'd, Gondamar againe receav'd & likt of, poperie hart'ned by admission of those vnknowne conditions of connivenc, the forces in the Pallatinat wth drawne vpon Spanish faith & promises, by wch the king's children lost their patrimonie, & more monie has beene spent in embassies & treaties then would have kept an armie to have conquer'd even their Indies, our ould fast frinds difhartn'd, &

our soveraigne that is now, expos'd to more danger then anie wisdome or councell could admitt.

In like cases our predecessors have beene sedulous for releife & reparation in such/ wrongs. the loss of the Counte of Pontiffe in the time of R[ichard] 2. was laid to B^p Wickham's charge for disswading the K[ing] from a timely aid & succor. the loss of the Dutchie of Mayne was a capitall crime in parliament obiected to De la Poole in the daies of H[enry] 6. for a single & vnwise treating of a marriage for that K[ing] in ffrance ; & the Pallatinat was loft by a like Spanishe entercourse.

what councell hath begott such power to forraigne agents, to procure libertie for papists, pardon for Preists & Jesuits, & to become sollicitors att everie tribunall of the goverment, for the ill affected subiects of the kingdome, & to prevent their punishments?

what grants of impositions, before croft, have been late past, & complain'd of heer in parliament, the least of wch in the time of E[dward] 3. would have beene iudg'd a heynous crime & capitall, aswell as those of Lyons & Latimer?

Parliaments have beene suitors to the [King] in the times of E[dward] 3. H[enry] 4. H[enry] 6. to beftow/ honors on some servants; & that wch was kept as the most sacred treasure of the State, now is set to sale, at wch posterne more have beene late admitted, then all the merits of the elders have let in these last 500 years. Soe tender were those times in the preservation óf that iewell, that it was made an article in the iudgment of de La Poole, that he had procur'd himself to be Earle, Marquess, & Duke of one & self same place, the like titles being vnquestion'd yet wth vs. E[dward] 1. restrain'd in pollicie the number of those that challeng'd it as due; & how the disproportion may now sort wth the reason of this state, cannot be well interpreted, when great deserts can have noe other recompenc then costlie rewards from the K[ing]. for now we are taught the vile price of that wch was once ineftimable.

Spencer, was condemn'd in the time of E[dward] 2. for displacing good servants about the K[ing], & placing in his followers & adherents, not leaving waie, as the record of that time saith, either in church or Commonwealth, but to such as fin'd wth him or his dependants; & we now/ see how such officers are dispos'd.

it was a sad hearing the last daie when the Lo. Tresurer did relate the great debts, ingagements, & present wants wch his Matie does sustaine, the noice wherof I wishe may be buried in these walls, least it worke courage in our enemyes, dishartning to our frinds. it was noe small motive in the time of H[enry] 3. to banish the king's half brethren for procuring the king's wante; & Gaveston & Spencer for the like had the like fortune in the time of E[dward] 2. Michael de la Poole the ffather of the D[uke] of Suffolk, amongst other crimes, was ad-iudg'd for turning the subsidies that were granted not to their proper ends; & Wickham that great B^p was put vpon the mercie of his prince, for wasting in time of peace the revenew of the Crowne, to the yearlie oppression of the people. & the like offices were obiected to the ruine of the last D[uke] of Somersett.

too frequent are the examples in this kinde that shew the abuse of ministers. such improvidenc & ill councell led H[enry] 3 into soe/ great a straight, as he did pawne part of his dominions, ingagd all the iewells of the Crowne & those of St Edward's shrine at Westminster, not sparing, as it's said, the great Crowne of England. but above all was that lowe ebb of H[enry] 6. occasion'd by his favorit de la Poole, as it's exprest by Gascoine in his storie of that time, wch I have found heer since our comming to the meeting, who tells, that the king's revenewes were soe rent, as he was forc't to live, *de talijs & quindenis populi.* that the K[ing] was growen indebted *quinquies centena millia librarum.* that that favorit in treating a forraigne marriage, had lost a forraigne Dutchie. that to worke his ends he had caus'd an adiornment of the parliament *in villis & remotis partibus regni,* wher the people, *propter defectum hospitis & victualium,* few should attend, & soe enforce those few, to vse that author's words, *concedere regi quamvis pessima;* & when an act of resumption was desir'd (that iust & frequent waie of

Page 248.

reparation for the State, w[ch] from the time of H[enry] 3. to E[dward] 6. all kings but one did exercise)/ that great man then oppos'd it, & tould the K[ing] it was *ad dedecus regis*, & soe stop't it. but what succeeded in the parliament? the same author tells y[u], that the Commons, though wearied wth travaile & expences, protested that they would never grant an ayde vntill the K[ing] should, *actua·liter resumere*, all that was belonging to the Crowne; & that it was *magis ad dedecus regis*, soe to be ingrost by the Counsell of one man, who had brought such miserie to the kingdome [and] such povertie to the K[ing]: on whom an act of exilement being made, the Act of resumption forthw[th] followed it, & immediatlie the supplie. if we should now seeke a paralell for this, how would it hould to vs? the revenewes all vasted & anticipated, as the Lo. Tresurer ha's confeft, that nothing does come from thenc for the present vse & maintenanc, hardlie anie thing can be look't for: the debts as excessive if not more, w[ch] we sawe latelie one man's arithmatick could not number. what has beene exhausted from the people, *in talijs & quindenis*, is too knowne, in the too wofull & lamentable experience/ of late times. what was lost for the Spanish match & treatie, children can speake, that were not borne to see it: by whom was caus'd the adiornment to this place, & for what ends, ther needs noe prophecie to tell vs. soe as in all things the cases are the same if that our acts be answearable. 'tis true presidents are noe Gods, yet some veneration they require. the honor of antiquitie is great, though it be not an idoll, & the wisdome of examples is most proper, if it be well applied. What was fitt at one time, all circumstances being like, cannot be said [to be] vnfitt, vnconvenable in another. noe threatnings may deter vs, nor yet difficulties, from the iust service of our Countries. our ffathers had not a greater trust then we, their reasons & necessities were not more. therfore I move, to pursue that remonstranc to the K[ing] & in due time we shalbe readie to supplie him.

this inflam'd the affection of the house, & pitcht it wholie on the imitation of their ffathers. the cleer demonstrations that were made of the likeness of the times, gave them like reasons, who had/ like interests & freedoms. but the Courtiers did not relish it, who at once forsooke both their reason & their eloquenc, all their hopes confifting but in praiers, & some light excuses that were fram'd, but noe defenc, nor more iustification was once heard of, in wch soft waie the chancelor of the Exchequer did difcourse. that the diforders wch were spoken of were not of that king's time, but brought in vnder the goverment of his ffather, & such as peace & quiet had begott. that in the K[ing] that was they had the virtues of his person, the promise of his word to assure their hope of reformation, if they would expect it till next meeting. therfore he desir'd those diftasts might be left off, & the present remonstranc that was talkt of; &

such an answear to be fitted for his Matie as the gentleness of his message, & sweetness of his nature did require. but finding by the inclination of the house, that that way could not serve, he concluded in another for the question of supplie, & prest to have a resolution in that pointe. that rocke was seene betimes, & therfore as speedilie avoided; for the negative the wiser sort did fear, the affirmative all generallie/ did abhorr. therfore in this wch requird little eloquenc or art, much was said on both sides, & much contestation was vpon it, wherin the new elect for Yorkshire Sr Thomas Wentworth by a new returne then come did soe well express himself for his countrie, as it desir'd that choise, & allai'd much of the labor to the contrarie. Sr Edward Coke also & others that did follow him, had the same power & reason. they wholie did decline the putting of the question, wherin still some instance being made, Mr Glanvile, that pregnant westerne lawier, did appease it, yet not by consent, but resolution of the house. he prest, that as a deniall were dishonorable for the K[ing] a grant wth difficultie were as disadvantagable for themselves, taking off all meritt from the act & by a metamorphosis converting it to that *panis lapidosus*, of the Ethicks. that such questions were not to be hasarded for princes, nor vsuallie propounded in that place, till the consent were manifest. that it was the prerogative of kings to call parliaments at their pleasure, but in counterpoise of that their ancestors had erected the priviledg for themselves to treat of what business they should pleasure. that to be putt vpon/ that question, was preiudice to that libertie, & the importunitie therin an implicit concession of an error in the calling to that place. Should the parliament spend, as by computation it does alwaies—9000^{li} a day, & that but for the grant of—40000^{li} in all? by crowning such councells wth success, we shall give encouragment to our adversaries. thus he declar'd him self, & concluded for the remonstranc to the K[ing] wth some forme of protestation for their meanings, that they did not then denie, but in due time they would supplie him. something was added vnto this by Sr Robert Mansell in answear to that wch was pretended for the Councell, who vtterlie difclaim'd all knowledg of the action, or anie consultation had vpon it: but said ther had beene some meetings, & some propositions spoken of for the navie, but noe designe, nor enterpries & soe noe counfell or advise. vpon this all color was remov'd from those that sought the question. noe such question could seeme proper, wher ther was noe reason for supplie. the supplie could not be hop'd for in an action wth out Councell, wch being in doubt before, then in full credit & beleife, that long debate concluded for a remonstranc to the K[ing]./ whilest the remonstranc was preparing, new complaints came in of the spoiles & insolencies of the pirats, & of divers cruelties wch were fuffred by the captives they had taken. the Turks were still roving in the west, the Dunkerks in the East, the cries came out of all parts, their losses great, their dangers more, their fears exceeding all, that noe marchant dar'd venture on the seas, hardlie they thought themselves secure enough at land! it was alledgd by some, that as the king's ships were stop't from going to releive them when it was order'd by the Councell, soe they were then, though readie on the coasts, or in the harbors neer them, wher those rogues were most infestuous, & nothing might be done. naie in some cases it was prov'd that the marchants had beene taken even in the sight of the king's ships, & that the Captaines being importun'd to releive them, refus'd their protection or assiftanc, & said they were denied it by the instructions wch they had. vpon wch it was conceav'd to be more then common negligenc. the Duke was thought faultie in this pointe, he being Admirall, from whom the instructions were deriv'd. for that he had the imputation of those/ errors, wch some did then terme crimes, and thervpon wch formerlie was forborne, he was then charg'd by name. this first direct nomination of the D[uke] done by S^r ffrancis Seymour, tooke off all visards & difguises in wch their discourses had beene maskt. then in plaine terms the ielosies were exprest, wch hindred the satisfaction of the K[ing]. his neerness to his Matie was toomuch, his greatnefs & exorbitanc offensive, his power & practise were both doubted & dislik't. in his person was contracted the cause of all those miseries. all the expressions & examples wch formerlie had beene heard of, were then applied to him. his faults & errors were the same, soe was desir'd his punishment, & that, wth the rest, likewise to be represented to the K[ing]. this putt new thoughts into the Court, how they might state their business, that though the[y] gain'd not, nothing might be lost, to wch end was

Page 255.

prepar'd a new message from the K[ing]. two things were therin aim'd at in favor of the D[uke] the first an act to prevent the remonstranc that was comming, wth wch Sr Henry Marten was entrufted, theother an answear in that point of Councell/ vnto Mansell, wch the king's Sollicitor had in charge ; & these for that worke, did wth all diligenc prepare them selves.

the next daie, when those parts were to be acted, some interruption did fall in by a double conferenc of the houses. the first concernd the petition vpon the pardon to the Jesuit, wch the Lords excusd onlie as a worke of the Ambassadors, for whom ther was an order made in Rome, that none must come, but wth one of those familiars to attend him, wch prest their masters as importunatly for their fellows, as they had prest the K[ing]. that the king's answeare late deliverd was a securitie for the future. that they likewise would all move him not to give passage to the like, wch they suppos'd might be as effectuall to the end, as the petition then intended, wherin they refus'd not to concurr, but said they crav'd onlie a consideration in that pointe. theother part was for some releife for London, wch they propounded to be done as by an ordinanc of parliament, that in soe generall a calamitie & distress, ther might be a generall contribution made towards it, wch being reported to the Commons had a present confir-/ mation & allowance, as in the former they alfo rested satiffied.

these things dispatch't, the message was delivered, that vrg'd the supplie againe to renew the former question.

wch meeting aswell wth wonder as opposition, that that question should be stir'd, wch was before resolv'd on, the ould artist makes his introduction from that ground, & thus beginns his part of the apologie. that ther were two extreames wch wisdome did avoid, theone *abrupta contumacia*, theother *deforme obsequium*. this being base, vnworthie of a man, that both vnpleasant & vnsafe. that the meane onlie was commended, & Lepidus for that soe magnified by Tacitus. that he wisht princes would desire nothing vnfit from subiects; but, if they did, he would have the deniall in such manner, as it should seeme not to their persons, but the things. he alledg'd that saying of Tiberius, that common men are rul'd by profit, princes by fame. that profit therfore being more considerable wth them, he would that way direct his reason, framing a dilemma thervpon. that either the monie disburst on the preparations had beene well spent or not. if well, that it was then noe husbandrie for want of a little to be added to lose somuch laid out; if ill, that not giving/ would excuse those ministers that imploied it. soe as in the first sence, it was vnprofitable *omni modo*, in the second *aliquo modo*, not to give, & therfore he wish't ther might be some respect of that. to dispute the necessitie at that time, for the manner how it was incurrd, he said, would be like that act of him who seeing another in the mire that cald to him for help, spent somuch time in questioning how he came thither, that before his hand was given, theother was sunck past hope. a necessitie ther was then, that was confest of all sides, therfore he vrgd, that their labor ought to be how for the

Page 258.

present to releive it; what kinde of necessitie it was, & how that necessitie was incur'd, might be confiderd of therafter.

from thenc he descended to his more perticular bufinefs & confest in generall that the kingdome was in sickness & needed phisicke, & that he lik't the medicines that were spoken of, but doubted that those dogdaies were vnseasonable to applie it. that having the king's assuranc for a new meeting & full opportunitie therin, he wish't rather to deferr it till that time, least opening the wound onlie they should make it more incurable. manie things he propounded of that kinde, but not wth/ such success as was expected. Page 259. some did imagine that an act of expiation to the Court for the former trespass he had done, not a will offering, & what properlie was his owne, & in that regard gave the less credit to it. more it did lose the Advocat, then anie waie made advantage for his Client, whose fame was not better by that art, theothers worse. the like fortune mett the other, who handled that particular of the Counsell. wherin he made a long narration & discourse, how the Counsell had often mett, as was pretended by the D[uke], how Sr Robert Mansell did wth draw himself vpon privat reasons & distasts; how divers perticulars were propounded & debated by the rest, & the designe in question by them all resolv'd on. how the Lo. Chichefter, had left some papers that commended it; how Sr Edward Cecill, who was acquainted wth the secret, & best could iudge vpon it, had said it was probable, & an ould plott of the prince of Orange's. other things of this nature he produc'd, more coloring the conclusion. the Lo. Chichester being dead, & the truth of the papers being vncertaine, that wrought but little on the iudgment of the Audienc. Sr Edward Cecill a commander for the action could not but manifer/ the designe, therfore was that assertion thought as invalid as the other, neither authenticke for satiffaction in the proofe. from the rest of the Councell ther came nothing, who were all living, & some ther : & yet if their attestations had beene brought, such a command has greatnes, as some men would have doubted, though others had beleev'd.

after this some other loose arguments being made to revive the question for supplie, wherin some presidents being vouch't by him that had decried them ; as those of 29. &. 31. El[izabeth] &. 3. Ja[mes]. wherin augmentations had beene made to the grants then first resolv'd on ; whenc was infer'd a perswasion for the like: a replie it had which was a Colophon to the pointe, comming vnexpectedlie from a gentleman, that had ther never spoke before, but by that became first knowne for his abilitie, who being a Lawier, & but younge, more studied then yet practis'd in the affaires of that assemblie, or the world, thus made his initiation to that service, and his discoverie vnto either.

Mr Speaker, the question in debate is whither to give or noe, & therin my opinion is absolute, not to give. for wch before I declare my reasons, I will make some/ answears to the arguments on the contrarie, wherby the worth of both may more easelie appeer. ffirst ther has beene an obiection made against insifting on ould presidents, & that we should not make them Gods, wch in part was aunswear'd, that they were venerable, though not idolls: but further, presidents are the life & rule of parliaments, noe other warrant being for the parliament it self, for the authorities it pretends to, then the extent vse & practise, wch is drawne out by presidents. & should not then parliaments be carefull to preserve that rule inviolable, to make it constant like it self? in other Courts differenc of presidents are badges of distemper & weakness in those times, much more would it be in this great Court of Parliament, wch being the rectifier of others, should this waie doe it self; & if that straie or wander by wch the rest are guided, who shall then rectifie & reduce it? but even those that speak against them, doe most magnifie & endear them when they/ thinke them vsefull to them selves. for when reason has forsaken them, as in the agitation of this question, how have the[y] strain'd for presidents to be assiftant to their arguments? as those of .29. & .31. El[izabeth]. & .3. Ja[mes], wch yet were most different from this case, & make nothing in the pointe. ffor that of 29. El[izabeth] was onlie thus. that after such time as the subiects had given to that good Q[ueen] of ever famous memorie, one subsidie & two fifteenths, vnderstanding by hir councell that she was to make great preparations for a warr to resist that invincible armado in 88. they by their Speaker tould the Q[ueen] that they had gone as farr for that

Page 262.

time as they could, but if she had occasion, they would shortlie supplie hir againe, where vnto she gaue that answear (w^cb I wishe likewise they would register in their memories & represent it to the K[ing]) that she would first search the bottome of hir coffers before she would greive hir subiects. wher now is the advantage of this president, wch somuch is stood on? nothing was done in this of that wch we are presd to. but they'le suppose it/ promis'd; noe, nor that, but rather the contrarie is insinuated. they refus'd then to make an addition at that time, &, not vnlikly for the reason of their priviledg. that wch was promis'd, was wth referenc to another time & meeting; soe as this confirmes the infiftanc wch we make, & does noe way impeach it.

but the next, 31. of that raigne; what was then added was before the act was past & vpon the excessive charge laid out for defenc against the Spaniar'd, or rather to congratulat that divine victorie & deliverance, when was the first time that euer two subsidies past at once. & for the like summe now I wishe we had like occasion.

that of K[ing] J[ames] was in the same manner introduc'd, not when the act was past, but while it stood in the pleasure of the house, & soe some others might be reckon'd, wch sort not wth our case but shew what our predecessors did heerin, & I doe hope that we shall doe the like. But the lawe of necessitie has beene vrg'd; & though answear'd, this more it shall receave. if ther be such a necessitie as is said, why should not his/ ma*tie* be willing that we should now redress it? Page 264.

waies have been propounded, & more I know would be, if that libertie were admitted, soe to supplie this necessitie & all others, & give the [King] subfistanc, as his predecessors had before him, to be both lov'd & feard. was ther yet never the like necessitie before this for fower hundred years & more, in wch we have light from parliaments? surelie ther have beene farr greater causes then is now, & yet noe such president can be found. But ther ha's beene a strange argument made *ab vtili*, that it is profitable to give, *argumentum cornutum*, by way of dilemma to enforce it, that either the former monies spent in the preparation have beene well laid out or not; if well, why should we not pursue it; if otherwise why should we take the fault vpon ourselves by refusing to add a little, & therby be difabled to call the delinquents to accompt? by the reason of this argument the parliament should be bound to mayntaine all actions & designes; for either they are good or not, & by that rule we should give the sword vnto our enemyes for the ruine of our selves. ffor the calling/ of the actions of that great man to question, who knowes not that nothing can be done wth out permission of the K[ing]? & if soe, it may be aswell wth out supplie as wth it, it being not the manner of great princes to make marchandise of their iustice. much has beene said vpon the answear Page 265.

of our petition for religion, & manie lines drawne thenc to the intention of this business, as if religion were the servant, this the mistris. I am as glad of the answear in it self as anie member of the house, though I am sorrie to this purpose it is vs'd. but who knowes what fruit ther will come from it? naie, we have cause to fear it, when the protestation is not answearable to the fact. the pardoning of Jesuits, protection given to Papists, support & countenanc to Arminians, even at this time, shewes more then common danger. why shall we not therfore desire the K[ing] the lawes may be executed on recusants? wch if he would command, & that, reallie, to effect it, they might be all convicted at the next assise or sessions, & then, by that means, ther would be monie to supplie him wth farr more then is demanded./ Henrie the fifth was a wise & potent prince, not inferior to anie since the conquest, & yet what did his subiects vnto him? in the first year of his raigne they found a remisnefs in the execution of the laws. vpon wch they spake plaine language, & praied him then, in parliament, to putt the lawes in execution better then his ffather had done. w^{ch}, though sharp, was good & wholesome councell, & followd by that K[ing] wch likewise if his Matie will now doe, he may enioy like honor & prosperitie, & be both lov'd at home, & fear'd abroad. ther were some other arguments alfo vs'd, as that it is the first request ot'h K[ing]. that granting it wilbe an expression of our loves to him, denying a pleasing to the papists, wch may assoone receaue their answears; for the last, it is noe reason to perswade, for the Divell sometimes is consenting to good workes, though for ill ends he ha's. for the second, we must soe love the K[ing] as we neglect not the Commonwealth. we must remember the vnion is betweene them wch noe good subiects will divide. we must *amare et sapere*, not *depravari amore,*/ love to love alwaies, not to perish by our love, wch were not onlie an iniurie to ourselves but to the obiect of our love, the K[ing]. for the first we must consider what ill effects have follow'd the pressures of the people, wherin our stories mention nothing but tumults & commotions; the time is dead & all commerce shutt vp by the sickness heer at home, by the not car'd for piracies & robberies abroad. the charge alreadie laid in the two subsidies that are granted adds a great burden to the people. what more might doe we know not, but his ma^tie being wise, if he faile in this request, is better to be perswaded then a multitude. I might give other reasons against these, as that by the cafinefs of the subiects to supplie, princes become more careless of their revenewe & expence. that it may well be doubted in the frequent grant of subsidies, that they may turne in time & growe into revenew, as in Spaine & Naples those wch were voluntarie contributions are now made due & certayne; & the tonnage & pondage heer wth vs reckond in the ordinarie, wch at first was meant/ but for the garding of the sea, & soe the

Page 267.

Page 268.

acts still have it. But these things need not when our owne rules conclude vs, wch I desire we may observe, & soe pass on to the remonstrance that was ordered.

this put the Courtiers beyond hope, who sawe noe waie of saftie but retreat, & to that and continuall entercourse being made wth intelligenc to the D[uke], the Commission for dissolution of the Parliament wch was secretlie prepar'd, was forthw^th delivered to the Keeper, who according to the forme was to execute & discharge it.

Some difficulties this had caus'd in the deliberations of the Councell, wher it had beene oppos'd before the K[ing]. the Keeper heer againe had wth much earnestnefs declar'd himself, & wth manie reasons indeavor'd to disswade it: but his power was found to[o] weake, in contestation; for the others, the faction of that partie did prevaile; not y^t it spake more trulie but more pleasantlie. soe was that sceane contriv'd, that the D[uke] himself seem'd a suitor for the contrarie, & on his knees did deprecat that wch he moft desir'd. but the resolution was immoveable in the K[ing]. &, as none doubted, soe practis'd by the other, vpon w^ch/ the opinion of the Keeper was reiected, & not longe after that him self. the Commission being heard of, wth the Commons wrought some diftraction in their mindes. those that were fearfull did encline to some accommodation & respect. those that were resolute, & had hearts answearable to their heads, insisted on their greivances; for w^ch, bicause the remonstrance was prevented by the shortness of the time, this protestation was compos'd, as a character of their meaninge.

We the Knights, Citizens, & burgesses of the Commons house of parliament, being the representative bodie of the whole Commons of this realme, aboundantlie comforted on his Maties gratious answear touchinge religion, & his message for the care of our health, doe solemnlie protest & vowe before God & the world wth one hart & voice, that we are all resolved, & doe heerby diclare, that we will ever continue most loyall & obedient subiects to our most gratious Soveraigne, K.[ing] Charles, & that we wilbe readie in convenient time, & in a/ parliamentarie waie, freelie & dutifullie to doe our vtmost indeavor to discover & reforme the abuses, & greivances of the realme & state, & in the like sort to afford all necessarie supplie to his most excellent ma^tie vpon his present, & all other his iust occasions & designes, most humblie beseeching our ever deer & dread Soveraigne in his princelie wisdome & goodness to reft assured of the true and hartie affections of his poore Commons, & to esteeme the same, as we conceave it is indeed, the greatest worldlie reputation & securitie a iust K[ing] can have, & to accompt all such, as slanderers of the peoples affections, & enemies to the Commonwealth, that shall dare to say the contrarie.

this was by the penne of Mr. Glanvile, who not long after had the[ir] thanks, & it was forthw^th read, & ordred to be presented to the K[ing] by his privie Councellors of that house. wch being so agreed on, & some loose motions made, for cleering those by the suffrage of the house, that were thought subiect to distaste for their expressions in that place; some/ such overtures being made, that were reiected as vnnecessarie, former experienc having prov'd them to be vfeless & vnprofitable; those things laid aside, & the vsher of the black rod admitted wth his fatall message to the house, the Speaker left his chaire, & being attended by the rest, went presentlie to the Lords, wher the Commission was then read, & soe dissolv'd that parliament.

this dissolution, though thus wrought, gave not in all things satiffaction to the Courtiers, though in some they had content. that they were freed from the Constellation that was over them, & the dire aspect it had vpon the corrupt matter of their works, seem'd as a happiness in part; but they still fear'd the influenc, & the future operation it might have; &, for the present, they had fail'd in their expectation & designe. on theother side ther was not less trouble to the Countrie, as the intelligenc did dispers. that saving of their monie did not please, as the demand dislik't them. all men possest their neighbours, that that meeting was the Duke's. that he to color the follie of his enterprises had practis'd to entitle them to the Parliament. that, the Parliament difcovering his practise & corruption, to secure himself therin, he had raisd a ielosie in the K[ing], by wch that breach was made. this was beleev'd of all; & manie revolutions itt did cause in myndes not well compos'd. that suddaine alteration, & great change, from extremitie to extremitie, was more then vulgar stomacks could digest.

the great hope they had conceav'd, to be wither'd in

the Spring, cast a blacke face of sorrowe over their whole affections. this to be done by him from whom the contrarie was expected, added to that an anger. divided betweene these, their thoughts and times were spent, while the others, not less passionat, were in studie for themselves. manie things were obnoxious vnto them, made them, even, obnoxious to themselves. the prefent preparation of the ffleet, & the eye the world had in it, wch could not be prevented, or declin'd. the future expectation of a Parliament, and the satiffaction should be given it both for the ffleet/ & them (for as they were conscious to themselves of the publicke iniuries they had done, wch they heard cal'd vpon at that meeting, & could not doubt they would be forgotten in the next ; soe they could prophecie for theother what success should follow it, iudging either by their counsells or themselves) these things therfore were a terror in their harts running through all their motions: yet the ffleet must be sett out, that formerlie was resolv'd on, & the D[uke] was held too pretious to be adventur'd in the voiage, whenc nothing but loss & dishonor could returne ; however the Commission that was granted him must stand, that what glorie could be had, (as all such expeditions afford some in their entranc & beginnings) might be added to his trophies. & what the *exitus* might import, ther was another nam'd to ffather it, for whom likewise a Commission was dispatcht of the same power & latitude, but subordinat to the other. this substitute was Sr Edward Cecill, brother to the then E[arl] of Exeter, a man whom years & experienc might have squar'd

Page 273.

Page 274.

for better purposes &, imploiments. his whole time/ & studie had beene spent vpon the warrs. he then retain'd, in the service of the States, the command of a regiment of ffoote. his respect wth them, for the qualitie of his blood, was noe detraction to his meritt. his carriage and deportment were not ill, his presence good, his conversation full of affabilitie & courtship; & in his affections ther was doubted nothing that was corrupt: facility was the greatest preiudice he was subiect to, wch rendred him credulous & open to those that were artificiall & obscure, wherby he became exposd, & subservient to their wills, & was drawne to tread those paths wch themselves refus'd to walke in.

his Commission stil'd him, in the presence of the D[uke] Lo. Marshall of the feild, the D[uke] by land & sea, being appointed Generall; but in his absence it did make him Generall, as himself, vpon wch ther arose an adulation in the Court, that was not wth out laughter to the Soldiers, the [Duke] for superexcellenc being term'd Generalissimo in their dialect, & the other Generall; soe as this had at noe time less then was his due, that, as in all things els, had more./

this being setled for the ffleet, a *Consulto* likewise followd it, how to accommodat for the Parliament. nor was, in this, the businefs, for retraction of the errors, but for prevention of complaints. the ould courfes must continue, wth out anie lessening of the exorbitance, onlie the studie was that noe man might oppose it; & to that end a proiect was receav'd to remove the moft active of the Commons, those that had then diclar'd themselves, charging them wth imploiments that might make them vncapable of the Parliament, presuming therby others would be deter'd, & the whole abilitie of that house extracted wth those persons, soe as noe man should remayne of knowledg or affection to contest them. Soe shallow are those rivelets of the Court, that they thinke all wisdome like their murmure. kingdomes they will measure by the analogie of their rules; but in this they deceave themſelves, as in all other things the world, & as they iudge of kingdomes, kingdomes may iudge of them. great is the varietie in a kingdome both of knowledg & abilitie. great is the varietie/ of persons, & of their studies & exercises to acquire them. the formes of wisdome are as various as are mens. as one is bould, & active, another wilbe cautious & reserv'd. this plotts, that speaks, a third iudges & discerns; & in all these some are excellent, yet appeer not, while their works are done by others, but are content & happie to be shadow'd in themselves; all difficulties being declin'd, dangers prevented, & their desires made good : yet againſt all, wher necessitie shall require, they will & are readie to stand forth. Soe did it prove in this, contrarie to the prediction of the Court: but their conclusion held proportionable to their iudgment, by wch that proiect was approv'd, some being design'd for sheriffes then at home, others for other imploiments further off, wherby they thought themselves sufficiently secur'd, & on that securatie being setled, from their resolutions in these things, they then betook themselves to other entertaynments more at Large./

Page 276.

ILLUSTRATIVE ADDITIONS

FROM

SIR JOHN ELIOT'S UNPUBLISHED MSS.

AT PORT ELIOT.

1

SUPPLEMENT.

(Continued from Vol. I. p. 173.)

NOTHER memorable Speech in the same Parliament against Supply is wholly in Eliot's own handwriting, thus:—

"Our English nation has a great fame, for wch we rest in- Fol. 40-41. debted to our ffathers: & nothing has been more fortunat exord. to vs then ther examples when we have observd them, nothing more vnhappie then our waies, when we have wandred in those paths that were not trodden to vs. I could demonstrat this by many things either of peace or warr, if I would vse digression, but the matter now in hand sufficiently will prove in what difficulties we have mett, what p̄iudice we have had beyond the fortunes of all former times since we have declin'd their rules; how short *narrat.*

we come of the happiness of their labors, even in this place; & how we have formd a way, almost a beaten way, to make the meetings fruitless. their manner was in their assemblies, as their records informe vs, first to consult of publicke business, to prepare good lawes, to represent their greivances, to dispatch those things that concern'd the Country, to make knowne their state: then, when they fownd, how they were enabled, how they were releivd; when noe oppressions feard them, iustice was equall, the lawes open to all, commerce at liberty, all trade free; then, then they did thinke of monye, then did treat of giving, & were not wanting in such summs as fitted wth those times, fitt for the occasions of the state, the honor of their sover. this course as it mayntaynd the dignity of their gifts, to have y^m soe expected, & often gave y^m a reputation, especially wth strangers, before the summs were knowne, beyond their proper values: soe it secur'd their proceedings in the rest free from interruption, & both gain'd the benefitt of time, & that advantage wch the hope of monie alwaies has afforded. how this practise has beene declind by vs it's manifest in the effects have followd it. wittness decimo octavo, witness vicesimo primo of King James, witness the first of our sover. that now is, witness the next, witness the last in all wch. as now, we were importun'd to precipitat: dangers were obiected, necessities alledgd, & (those prevailing) did they induce any thing in consequence but against vs? examine them, particularly that in 18. the first president of such hast, when two subsidies were granted, granted in the beginning of a parl: granted wthout a session, (a grant never knowne before) granted vpon promise not to be vrged againe or vsd as an example, did it not prepare the way for the next parl : was it not followd ther ? & what rendred it to the sub^{ts} in the continuance of the same ? after that turn were servd nothing but distasts, checks to their proceedings, reiections to their suites, questions to their priviledges, punishments threatend to their members, & those aswell sitting the house as when it was dissolvd, wch in part nott long after was performd, the rest has beene acted since; things as new and strange to the ould times, as were such hastie grants, the fitter to attend them. in 21mo the copie of that good patterne, when 3. subsidies. 3. fifteenes were given (wch bounty we had hope would have servd long) did it not still endear the manner, & as hastily draw in the demand in the next year, in the next parl : ? & then when we had as willingly consented, & presumd to have satisfied in the same sitting, & from thenc followed vs, or rather drave vs vnto Oxford ? having dissolvd vs ther, & many waies disperst vs, when we were calld againe in the next parl : was it forgotten then ? was it not reinstanct? supplie y^u know was the mayne thing proposd, & that soe strickly as if nothing els were necessary, for that we were presently putt vpon disputes, we were prest to resolutions w^{ch}, (however large & honorable beyond proportion of all former times we had accorded) being (yet) secretly adulterated & traduct, renderd vs suspected, distastfull to his Matie. & by that exposd vs to all the miseries & calamities wch we have sufferd since. come we yet neerer, come to this ꝑsent parl : we sitt in, in the last session wch made an indication of such hope vpon our good agreem^t wth the K. wherin the knot & obligation was soe tied as it was by all men thought inviolable: the K. having cleerd our liberties to vs, we having granted a retribution to the K. wch no sooner had beene past vs but y^u know what an alteration was then found : what answear we receavd to our Remonst. & wth what passages to endear it : what catastrophe what caulupon we then had, of wch I must conclude as Cicero did in the lines, *nolo rem eam commemorando renovare cujus omnino memoriam omnem tolli funditus ac deleri oportet,** such have been the effects of all those hasty givings. now comes the like demand, the like request in the like time, like reasons to induce it, like necessityes pretended, what shall we now doe ? shall we give lesse then formerly we have done ? that wilbe said a shortning [of] affections to his Ma^{te}, a neglect of his affaires, a neglect of common good, naie (I doubt not) but from these late practices 'twilbe vrgd a breach of president too ; & shall we in all these make our selves obnoxious ? yes ; to those that soe conceive it, those that soe applie it, but to the truly wise, the iudicious, the vnderstanding man, the man of rectified & clear senc it wilbe otherwise ; to him it shall appeer encrease of our affections to our soveraigne, tender of his affairs, care of common good & reformation of those ill examples latelie introduct. ffor as we have seene of all these hastie givings the effects, the reward, miserable & vn-

---

* Cicero Pro P. Quintio, 21, 70. " Tametsi nolo eam rem commemorando *renovare*, cujus omnino rei memoriam omnem tolli funditus ac deleri arbitror oportere."

happie; soe to the King & State, from the same presidents, if they be well considered you shall likewise finde them fruitless & vnprofitable. for first that in 18°. given as y^u may remember to a good end, & soe desird, the defenc of the Palat: (o^h would it had beene well defended) what wrought y^t supply? what conclusions did it bring to the worke intended? what advantage gave it to the cause? none I can call to minde: the success saies none, & from thenc wth reason we may better thinke those monies interverted then any waie imploid to soe good a vse. sure I am (& wth greif I speake it) the Palat: is lost, & as ffame reports it, for want of succors & releife from vs. the next in 21mo when a larger contribution was made, the largest that ever was before, the ends set downe for wch it was appointed, provisions made how to be dispos'd, what came of that? did it effect any thing worthy the honor of the King, or state? surely noe; nothing that was visible; nor doe I thinke the monies issued for the ends proposd, but drawne some other waie, for wch when it was requird last parl: they could not be accounpted:

By the next the first of our Sover. that now is, had the State any encrease or profit it retaynes? the consequence saied otherwise, & rather shewed the necessity made larger then any way retrencht, wch was apparant in that not long after were pursued the vnheard of proiects, infallible arguments of extreame necessity: I might likewise instanc ye last, of wch noe man can be ignorant it is soe new: what advantage it has wrought, every man may iudge: that the necessitie continues their demand does prove, for notwthstanding all these aides wch soe speedilie have beene gotten, those things &c̃. . . . as my weake memory, & this time would give me leave, I have suddainly observd vpon our new waies our new manner of promising, of granting subsidies, in the beginning of a sitting wherof we againe deliberat to day. I have shewd y^u in the whole practise how disadvantagable they have been to vs; I have given y^u from the particulers part of the preiudices we have had. I have likewise shewd y^u towards the King how little profit they conferrd, how little his estate, how little his affaires are better by them, let me add this too, what riotts, what excesses, what insolencies, what evills, it may be feard they have causd in other men. & then consider whether it be now fitt we should doe the like againe. we have ever lovd our princes; & shall alwayes doe soe; we have beene still willing to supply them, & are ready now : but for the manner let it be according to the customes of our ffathers in the ould formes, wth wch we were soe happie, & for the quantity, let it not be doubted, but as our love exceeds, that shall hould proportion. for the reputation & creditt soe many waies idolatrizd, let this suffice : nothing soemuch confirms it, nothing somuch augments it as an agreement heer, the correspondenc wth the parl : the confidenc, the assuranc in his people will more magnifie the King, then all the treasures of the whole kingdome drawne into his coffers. that invaluable iewell of the sub^{ts} harts is above all account. soe Alexander esteemd it. Therfore I desire that this proposition may heer rest, & that our supply may be the better when it comes, my motion shalbe that we may now goe on in matters to enable vs."

A short but pungent Speech succeeds this upon close of the Lawyers' arguments on behalf of Liberty of the Person. It follows :—

"M^r Sp^r

Vpon this grave deliberation wch has beene in that great pointe of libertie, I know not whether my affectation or admiration should be greater: affectation that by the arte & industrie of these gentlemen (whose profession speaks their excellence) the long obscurd & darkend rights 'oth subiect are laid open : admiration, that to the heigth of argument & witt ther has' beene vsd such modesty & sweetness, as in vindicating the infringd liberties of the subiect we can but seeme to effect the advantage and greatness of his Ma^{te} & in the cleering of our owne interests to have noe other end, but to make our selves more worthy the service of our Soveraigne, wherin let me give y^u this observation by the way, & I shall desire those gentlemen that have enter course at Court to take it thither wth them, that the glorie of noe K. was ever weakened by the multitude of bondmen but in the number of free subiects consists the honor of the Soveraigne : such have been our ffathers & such I hope we & our children shall continue.

this dispute has beene of two different parts drawne from the Severall reasons of the parties. the one of arguments for the liberty of the sub^t, the other conteyning answears & obiections made against them. the arguments for the sub^t, had two principall grounds they stood on, two generall foundations vpon which divers perticular superstructions

Fol. 42-44.
4 Car. reg.

S^r. Ed. Coke.	were erected, & those that hono^{ble} person (whom posteritie must thank for the large characters of his virtues) wch in their service he has exprest, calld his *duo instrumenta, ratio & authoritas,* on wch grounds were laid such curiosities of structure for the libertie & freedome of the sub^t, & of such proportion in varietie of reasons, in multitude of cases, diversitie of Lawes, multiplicity of presidents in pointe, that wthout further examination or triall they had beene an evidenc sufficient for the cause. But to follow the exact Justice that was vsd in the equall hearing of all parties on the other side, what reason was product, what case vouch't, what law, what president alleadged wch had not their full answear or were conceavd not worth it? for reason y^u know the King's Counsell confest himself & stood vpon excuse, not vpon defenc of that wch has beene done. cases he gave none & for lawes he instanc't onlie that of
Wes^t: 1. cap. 15.	Westminster expounded to his senc by Stamsford, w^{ch} (the contemporaneous expositions mention'd by that great sage 'oth Lawe; the vnderstanding of the former & latter times of the scope of Magna Charta, soe exquisitly retrivd out of the most hidden & obstruse corners of antiquitie by my most learned frind, & the exposition of those other lawes that were descendants from that great mother & made onlie in explanations of the same, naie the verie words & meaning of Stamsford himselfe well collected by
Mr Rolls.	my honest Counteyman) doe soe fully answear as I presume ther rests no difficulty therin. ffor presidents, ther
13. Jacob Saltingston.	was only insisted on that of 13°. Ja. wherin some advantage was supposd, for wch I shall desire y^m to observe but

these 3 pticulars. the authoritie it had, a yonge students notes & some privat observations he had taken. 2. the sufficiency therof, erring, as y^u know, in two most mayne pticulars vpon the recitall of the case of 34°. El. for wch we have the contradiction of an originall & authenticke booke of that great Lawier Anderson, one of the Judges of that time vnder his owne hand writing. 3. the reputation of the bringer, who y^u know likewise faild in the number wch he promisd & in the copie of the record that was p̃sented soe as if y^u compare & putt all things of all sides into the Scale of Justice, & their weigh *causâ cum causa, res cum re, ratio cum ratione*, as Cicero does direct: in the one part of the ballance y^u shall finde nothing but aer & lightness, in the other a full gravitie & weight. & now having thus given y^u the senc of what is past, let me add something more pticularly of myne owne that in this case of the libertie of persons I may not seeme lesse affectionat then others, as my former wants therin give me not less occasion to be sensible. Wherin I shall observe for the power that is exercis'd & pretended 3. pticulars more then formerly have beene toucht. 1. that it is against the law of nature, 2. the antient Ro. Civill Lawe, 3. that it is against the rules & maximes of pollicie: that it is against the Lawe of nature is implied by Plinie in the Embleame of the bees, wher the K only wants a sting as an instrument to hurt, that wher ther is power, ther should be least iniurie, & punishments should be the ordinances of the Lawes & not the acts of princes; but we have it fuller in that formula Ciceronis, that rule of Justice & the Lawe, wher he

34. Eliz. resolut. of ye Judges.

saies *detrahere aliquid alteri, & hominem hominis incommodo suum agere commodum magis est contra naturam quam mors* &c̃. What? is it soe to take any thing away? *detrahere facultates* (those things we call *bona fortunæ*, such as the philosophers soe willingly could leave that they might *citius philosophare?*) how much more then *detrahere libertatem*, wch is *detrahere lucem*, to take way the light nay to take away the life; for what life enioy we wthout light? what light wthout air, liberty? & therfore *a fortiori* it stands good, as air, libertie, is more pretious then are goods soe is that direption more contrary vnto nature. That it is against the Ro: civill law vnder whose authorities some have seemd to shrowde, besides the evidences given formerly out of that case of Pawle & those other inferences vpon that of the twelve tables *salus populi est sup̃ma lex* &c̃. Cicero likewise proves it in his *proprium civitatis*, wher he saies that *nihil de capite civis, vel libertate* &c̃. might be taken wthout the iudgm^t of the Senat or of them *qui de quâq̃ re constituti sunt iudices*. wch authority y^u see how full it is in pointe. I hasten what I may to give an end to this dispute, wch I thinke was formerly made soe cleer as it needs not further labor to conclude it. therfore I shall only mention & not argue new opinions. that this practise of Kings to imprison & comitt is against the rules of pollicie, appeers by reason also. for this rule admitts noe posterne, that *potestas humana radicatur in voluntatibus hominum*, & therfore subiects should be kept in affection to there Soveraignes: to wch end our lawes laie all faults & errors in the ministers, that noe displeasure

15°. Acts.

may reflect vpon the K. & soe Seneca does intimat, *regem debere solum prodeste nocere non sine pluribus*, & Machiavell that great master in this art, who was most indulgent vnto princes, & sought to advance all tyrannie, yet in this directs that they should disperse curtesies onlie by themselves & leave iniuries & punishm^{ts} to others, wch was also insinuated by the Antients in their fictions of Jupiter giving his thunders from the heavens whom they make *fulmen suum placabite solum mittere pernitiosum aliis tradere*, that wch was pleasant was his owne, that wch was distastfull came by others. these were the instructions of the Elders, these were the practises of those times: y^u see how both reason & iustice doe confirme it, & that it has a generall concurrenc of the law, vpon wch we may safelie heer resolve that what otherwise has beene acted was in preiudice of our rights, & then I hope we shall take such further course as may secure vs for the future."

Next comes a Fragment of his supreme Speech on the Miscarriages of the Reign :—

" Cales) wch was the first action of the King, & such first acts are not of least importance, when thervpon depends as Tacitus has observd it, the fame & expectation of the rest, honor & contempt taking their originalls from thence, wch seldome change & that not wthout great difficultie & adventure. in the first expedition vnto Cales, for wch such preparations had beene made, such immense provisions, such monie buried in the imploiment, what encouragement

Fol. 46.

from thence have we to render to the subiect? what grounds of perswasion for the like? y^u have heard too often what men & shipping have been lost as if they were made a sacrifice to our enemies: how our strength & saftie is impaird by that miscariage & adventure it is too knowne to all men, & that inestimable iewell of our honor, wch our ffathers prizd soe highly is therby crack't & blemisht: I dare not say tis broken, but the lustre of't is gone, wch makes vs less valuable wth our neighbours: that wch was our greatest riches beinge decayed. those great designes we know were vndertaken, if not made, by that great Lord the D. of Buckingham who assumd the name of generall, drew to him self the power & sole command of all things both for Sea & land: but y^u know he went not in the action. that for wch the whole kingdome must be troubled, was not thought worthie of his person, but a deputie & substitute must discharge it, wch what encouragement it may give to the affections of the people I leave to all men, that have reason, to determine it. before that the action of Count Mansfeld was soe miserable, and the men then sent soe managd, as we can hardly say they went: sure it is that nothing they did doe, & yet how few returnd here. that handfull likewise that was sent to the Pallatinat, not seconded, nor supplied, its knowne what ffortune they atcheivd. I might speake also of the action to Algiers & others of that nature, & who in all those had the Kings eare at pleasure, fashiond reports & propositions at his will: besides we might remember the treaties & negotiations that have beene, their infinit expence, & the nothing they returne but loss & dishonor to our nation; from whence such discouragments might arise out of the abuses of the ministers yet too potent, as should a supplie be wanting at this time it would iustlie make an apologie for the subiect. But leaving these things as forraigne & forgotten in the affaires at home, & the present administration of all business, what satisfaction, what liking can be renderd?"

Another fragment—also in Eliot's hand—against Mohun, deserves preservation:—

"The K^{ts}. Cit: & B. &c. having receavd from manie parts of the K^m. manie sad comp^{ls} of the great p^{r}ssures of the liberties & other iniuries intervinient, through the violenc & corruption of the officers to whose cares they are entrusted; & from the extreamest parts oth west beinge informd of most extreame oppressions: knowing wth all the pietie & goodness of his Matie, in the sunshine of whose favor they might rest vnder their vines & figtrees, & everie bee oth hive gather honie in that heat taking their severall pleasures of all the dainties of the feild, & consideringe that the abuse of serv^{ts}. does oftentimes reflect a preiudice to their masters; & even the beames of Matie. (that peice of wonder & admiration wch the common veiwe beholds not in it self, such glory being to[o] excellent an obiect for their sence) those beames I say are by the exorbatance of ministers (the clouds that interpose it) not seldome represented darkned & obscurd, & the straight line & rule of goverm^t it self renderd by such instrum^{ts} crooked & deformd: in contemplation of the honor of their Sover.

Fol. 47.

as of the welfare of his sub^{ts}. to cleer the brightnes of his Matie. from such mists & exhalations as ecclipse it; & to p^{r}serve & keep the reputation of his justice equall to his greatness, as famous to his frinds as fearfull to his enemies, they have desird this conferenc wth y^r lo^{ps} in w^{ch} (wth their true & hartie thanks for the continuanc of your respective correspondencie in all things & ready concession to this meetinge) I am commanded (though most vnworthie of that honor, most vnable to support it) to rep^{r}sent a charge against a member of y^r house ye Lo. M. whom avarice, ambition, iniustice, violenc, oppression, exactions, extorsions almost infinit, have made obnoxious to the cries & exclamations of the Countrie; wch vpon due examination they have found not lightlie to be movd & therefore have thought fitt to transmitt them to y^r lop^s, that having had like disquisition by y^r wisdomes they may receave such sentenc & definition as shall sorte wth the meritts of the cause & the satisfaction of y^r iustice, wch we know noe greatness can p^{r}vent. Wherin if the actions of the moderne & elder times may be drawne to likeness & comparison (as doubtless amongst manie vicissitudes & changes, ther are, at least, some fortunat concurrences in events) the intention they now have may not vnaptlie be resembled to that famous dedication of the temples of virtue & honor antientlie at Rome; for, as in that, the structure & formation had beene laid manie daies before by the great care & pietie of Marcellus whose fame therin remaynd; soe in this, that we shall now p^{r}sent, is the collection of a former time, (to wch though ther wanted opportunitie ther may not want acknowledgm^t) on the strength of whose foundations wee now build : & as in the other the crowne & glorie of the worke, the pfection, the dedication, was not admitted to Marcellus, yet granted to his sonne ; soe in this what was formerlie denied vs, in respect of opportunity, now, I hope we shall have the happiness to effect, & (wth that favor of y^r Lo^{ps}.) give it y^t conclusion wch shalbe acceptable, advantagable to all that owe their services & devotions to those most . . . . [a leaf of the MS. is here lacking, "those most" being catchwords] (for it was opend whiles this was in agitation in the Stanneries) & soe both stopping the further levie of the monie, & giving them opportunitie to exhibit their complainte.

Fols. 48-49.

W^{ch} complainte, as it was alledgd & provd to the Com^{te} y^u have now heard reported, wherin y^u have seene both the extension & execution of his power : in the extension both for the matter & forme, y^u have heard, what tinners he creats,* what priviledges he gives them, what effects they worke. in the execution, y^u have likewise heard his illegall preparations, his inequitable resolutions, his violent compulsions, his avaritious exactions ; & that last, more strange then all the rest, his Convocation ; wherin the calling, the proposition, the intention, the prosecution, the conclusion being noted wth the Time in wch all these things were done, (being wth in less then the compass of two years, a short space to make soe long a storie) this circumstance being noted wth the rest give it a full view & prospect for y^r iudgment.

it rests now only that I crave y^r pardons for my self,

---

* Cf. p. 128, l. 12.—G.

the pardon of the house, the pardon of the Com^te. that soe weakly have pformd soe great a worke & labord a report of this difficulty & length, wherin I must crave the assistance of my masters who made soe ill a choise that both for their owne honor & the service what my memorie or expression may have faild in, their more abilities will supplie.

[what more may be expected to enlarge it? would y^u compare it wth the moderne, would y^u measure it by elder times; what example can be found, what instanc can be given to paralell wth this? the iniustices, the oppressions, the exactions, the extorsions on the tinners, are soe infinit: the iniuries, the contempts, the scandalls, the abuses, to the Judges, to y^r Lo^ps, to his Matie, are soe great, that they may not vnaptlie be resembled to the antient warres of the Giants wth the Gods to give that fable truth. for in the preparation ther is laid Pelion vpon Ossa, insolenc vpon pride, covetousness on ambition, violenc vpon all: & in the acts themselves nothing can be seene but disdayne of Lawes, & contempt of goverm^t: not onlie to the depressing of the Commons but (as y^u have heard) to the scandall of y^r Lo^ps, naie to the p^riudice of the K. whose honor & advantage have noe supports soe sure as the lawes & liberties of the Kingdome, the inseperable accidents & adherentes of his Crowne & dignitie. And in this case y^r Lo^ps likewise may fitlié be compar'd to that great power of Gods that stood in succor of their Jupiter: for y^u are some Marse's, gods of Warr; y^u are some Apollo's, gods of wisdome, y^u are some Minerva's, excellent in both; y^u have a God of treasure likewise, a god of riches; & y^u have Mercuries,

Ambassadors; & of the Demigods, great officers great ministers to assist y^u : naie, y^u have a Neptune too, a god o'th Seas (wch is more then was granted by the Antients in the defenc of Heaven, or might formerlie have beene look't for heer wth vs : for of that ould deitie the fable tells y^u his affection to the giants, & the reason, *quoniam ex eius semine nati sunt*, they were of his begetting, of his breed, therfore he studied to support them, soe that noe help could be expected from his hands) but it is now otherwise, & a happie change is made : ther is now a Neptune, not of that allianc, whose aid y^u likewise have, wch does promise both assuranc & easiness in the victorie. I know my LL. in what high place he sitts; whom y^u must now encounter; I know the advantage he has gotten by being nombred wth y^r Lo^{ps}, wthall I know the integritie of y^r iustice, the sincerity of y^r worthe, wch noe respect, noe greatness can pervert, soe that ther needs not anie invitation or encouragement to be given y^u, more then y^r owne virtues & the great examples of y^r ffathers will present. I remember in the fiction that was made of the deifying of Claudius (who liv'd not the most excellent of men), it is said, that by the acquaintance & favor of Hercules he was secretlie admitted into heaven; but when the other Gods had taken accompt of his demeritts & found him not answerable to their worthes: to preserve the dignitie of that place, & the reputation of their order, he was by a sentenc of their Court, decreed incapable of that honor; & (notwthstanding the admission he had gain'd) adiudgd after thirtie daies to be expelld againe. I will make noe application what iudgment wilbe expedient for this Lo. the cause will best direct; the weight of that wilbe emergent in the proofes to wch for y^r more pertecular satisfaction I shall now refer y^r Lo^{ps}.

It rests my LL. that I now only crave y^r pardons for the manie imperfections I have made in this expression: my knowne weakness & infirmities, will, I hope, facilitat the excuse. the former favors of y^r Lo^{ps}, wch in this place I have receavd, & the obligation of that honor to wch these walls are witnesses, give me new assurance of y^r addition to that debt in perticular for myselfe; & that the errors wch have happen'd from my weakness shall not cast reflection on my Masters."]

As a companion to this, take another variant fragment in Eliot's hand, intended to have been spoken in the Lords' Conference against Mohun :—

Fol. 95.

" y^u may remember the old fable of the Giants that did warr agst the Gods & would drive Jupiter out of heaven. they made a preparation, they made an attempt, they brought it to a difficulty, in all wch y^u have it exampled in this case, the condition of this K^m, as if it were the reality of those fancies, or the destinie of this time, that we must now reduce that storie into act, & in favor of the Antients, give their fables truth. ffor first to answear the p^{r}paration, y^u shall finde heer, mountaine raisd on mountaine *pelion* vpon *ossa*. Arm̃ on pop[ery], in the C.[Commons] iniust., on opp. in the Comw. men for these corruptly brought to places, that by the example they might be ther corrupt: vast accumulations y^u shall see, immense suggestions of this Kinde, for strength & advantage to ther batteries; for facility & help to their ascent.

In the attempt likewise ye have a generall opposition of all goodness, all law, all libertie, all rell: the chaine by wch this fabrick is held vp, this K^m. is sustaind, how is it forct & strain'd? y^u know what is said of the golden chaine of Jupiter, that therby he was soe fastned to his throne, as noe powers could move him, & wth the same strength could drawe both earth & seas vnto him, all things by that attraction turninge readilie to his pleasure: that chaine wth vs is Justice, the equitie & pietie of our Love, iustice, both humane & divine, that same wch is *columna et corona reip, principium principis insigne: vnicum regnorum columen* as Pla. Aug. & Plu. terme it, & as Solomon, *that by wch all thrones & scepters are establisht:* therw^th. all things are drawne & vnited to our Jupiter; the earth, the Seas, the Elements, the whole masse & body of the k^m. & each parte & member in his sphear turning by affection & moving to his pleasure, naie God that moves them all & on whom all power depends, is therby linkt vnto him, & fastned to his aid; yet this chaine this strength they would dissolve, both by division & fraction in each parte, that by breaking the vnitie therof, they might likewise breake the entitie of this k^m: the linkes of wch it is composd consist of rell. & o^r lib: wth mutuall & reciprocall reflections involvd & woven in each other; in both wch they have attempted & sought by violenc, to force it. in rell. the lawes they have let downe to the purpose of our enemyes, & iustice made a sacrifice to their wills, not only in remission of the less penalties of pop. but in the highest &

greatest of their dangers, the forfeitures ye treason agst. their preists & Ies. & that vpon the bouldest & highest of their workes, the settling of their Coll. amongst vs & the evills incident to that. In libertie, all antient rights & priviledges neglected, naie the sacred rights & priviledges of this pl., & that not in a part or member, some pticuler of immunitye but in the generall, the whole; & that not by a transient act to impeach it for a time, but by a Judgm^t. positive & definit, wth the formes of all legalitye for ever to condemne it. ô the horror & execration it deserves, that they who have the *patronage* of iustice & tuition of the lawes, or rather, should be, (as more properly it were said) even the lawe & Justice in it selfe, should soe adiudge agst. all lawe & Justice & seeke to stop that fountaine from whence these streames doe flowe! this is truly, as one of themselves exprest in the passage of that iudgm^t, *exuere personam iudicis, et induere personam delinquentis;* or *sub persona iudicis agere delinquentem*, in the forme & figure of an Angell to act another parte. These are the Tytans (for soe Cicero calls all impugners of the lawe, not such as breake it [in] some points, but those that would ruine it in all) these make a warr agst. our Jupiter, & seeke the subversion of his K^m. by vndermining of rell: by vndermining of the liberties; by corrupting of his Justice & pietie, in these wch are the base & sure foundation wheron it does subsist.

& in the attempt, they have brought it to a difficulty, what eye sees not the hasard? how does the Ch. labor wth the danger she is in, & rell. shew her feaver? how does the Comw. suffer in his saftie, when his pillars are thus weakend?

constat vim Judicium non esse regiam M^{atem}. sed legum custodem &c. plat. p. 559.

& the indeavor cannot be, as formerly it has, to repaire the breach by par̃. but the indeavor of the par̃. (such is the exegēnc & necessity) must be brought to a compass of more straitness how to repaire herselfe. the difficultie, in either is apparant, I need not to dilate it, wch shews the danger, the chrisis we are in, & soe the resemblance likewise of this Giantlike attempt is continued in that pointe. the issue, I hope, wilbe the same and the same consequence shall follow it; the deiection of these Titans & the demolition of their works; the happiness & tranquillity of the K^m, the honor & securitie of the K.

that comes now in question, & is the subiect of this day, for wch y^r aides & assistances are crav'd : & to this end likewise we may well compare y^r L^{ps}. to that great power of Gods that stood in succor of their Jupiter. ffor y^u are some Marses, gods of warr; y^u are some Apollos, gods of wisdome; y^u are some Minervas, excellent in both; y^u have a god of Treasure also, a god of riches; & y^u have y^r Mercuries, Ambassadors; & of the Demigods, great officers, great ministers to assist y^u; what more can be thought needfull for defence? or expected in this aide? y^u are that full power wch antiently prevaild to support the throne of Jupiter, & have like abilitie at this time to maintaine the state & dignitie of o^r Sovr. wch against all assaults & machinations of these Titans, I hope will ever be impregnable." *

---

* Cf. p. 128, l. 5 (from bottom) onward as bracketed, which is crossed out in the MS. but retained, as offering variations of the text *ut supra.*—G.

SUPPLEMENT.

Now comes one of the great Speeches in the 2nd session of the 3rd Parliament after Buckingham's assassination by Felton. It is a privilege to be able to reproduce it :—

Folios 50 51.   "I presume y^u will easily beleeve what sad affections did possess me when wth y^r leaves & favors I last pted henc : I must heer acknowledg the like passions hould me now though in a different respect. when in observation of the times, I reflect vpon that thats past, weigh the p̄sent state & but looke towards the future, itt affects me wth terror and amasement, not in pticular for my self but generally for all, both wth sorrow & astonishment.

It is well knowne (noe p̄tence can pardon it) that in all our late actions forreign or domesticke, nothing is successfull; & in the forreign it is some doubt whether o'r tongues or swords have drawne the greater losses. By treaty we lost much, much in perticuler to ourselves, much to our allies (besides the reinforcment of our enemies) wch the daies of quiet did steale from vs ; and by our armes we have likewise lost, lost of our selves, lost of our allianc & still we are in losing our frinds, our ships, our men, (ô who has tears to number them, whose sorrowes can recount them wch in these late times have been lost) : our reputation, our honor is also gone, wch was the very secret of this nation & by wch even miracles have beene wrought : naie our religion is in hasard, not at home & heer; yet almost every wher abroad, & when that light is extinct in all the world besides I will submitt it to y^r iudgments how long we shall enioye it. our ffathers y\u207f know were happie, & we have seene felicity our selves, soe late it was amongst vs, when all our neighbours tooke comfort in our frindships : but now (such is the alteration, such is the change we suffer that) we are not only vnfortunat in our selves, but to our frinds disastrous ; an occasion of their miseries, but not of power to help them.

the Rhodians have a story of their Iland, that when Jupiter was delivered of Pallas it rain'd ther gould in great abundance, wch they morall thus. Pallas (soe borne) signifying both prowess & pollicy, martiall worth & wisdome, & that wisdome both human & divine implying not only information for the affairs of men but in the service & worship of the Gods, wch virtues (they say) being added to their Princes, their Jupiters, & by them made active, intimated in the delivery, they were alwayes prosperous & happie, full of the abundance of all wealth & honors ; w^{ch} . fable & morall my thinks may have iust application to vs, & some instruction for this purpose. Rhodes taken as this Iland, the proper seat oth Gods, wherin when action 'has' beene added vnto Counsell, & Counsell ioynd to action ; when religion & resolution have beene mett, what have we wanted, of that felicity or good wch wealth or honor could import? wisdome alone, Apollo has not satisfied, Mars has beene too weake, but both their virtues meeting wth religion & concurring in that center (as in the person of one Pallas) never have faild in all our chronocles & stories to give vs both riches & reputation, the true showers of gould mention'd in the fable, wherin ther is one thing more observable not vnworthie of the Antients, that this Pallas, this excellencie, this nurse of happiness & felicity, was not begotten by Jupiter in himself, but first conceavd by Metis (wch signifies Counsell) and being by her made ready then resumd by Jupiter into his owne head, & soe brought foorth. has our Metis, now, our Counsell beene pregnant in this age? have the children of these times beene like to her Minerva? in the late daies of peace we were all treaty wthout action, Mercurie was delivered, & y^u know what effects it had ; in these now Mars y^u see is borne whose successes are as ill ; but in all what Pallas is discovered, what Palladium can be found? wher has beene y^t center of religion to wch their motions should have turnd? what large circumferences have beene made vpon the extension of that pointe? if ther should be a strickt accompt therof taken in perticulars, I beleeve, ther would be found the like addition to their items, as Timotheus made for ffortune, & in this Metis had noe share. noe S^r. it is too manifest & in some it is acknowledgd, in others not deniable, that not Metis, but a wrong mother first did breed them, & from her fals conceptions have proceeded all these abortive issues we complaine of. But perchance it wilbe said that mother is now dead, the fear of that is gone, therfore heerafter it wilbe better, we may now resume new hopes; & thus I presume many men conceave; but for my part I cannot yet discerne it (& shall never stick to render my doubts open to this house, from whose wisdome only I must looke for satisfaction) though our Achan be cutt off the accursed thing remaynes;

the babilonishe garment is yet left wch Achan first brought in, & whilest that is wth vs, what hopes or expectations can we have? While the papists, the Arminians, & their Sectaries have countenance; while these men are in favor, while such are in preferment; while they stand so neer the elboe of the K. that they have power, (& in their owne cases) to impeach the creditt of this house, how can it be but the men of Aye must chase vs & god will not be turnd from the feircness of his wrath: for from thenc it comes that we are soe vnfortunat, vnfortunat abroad, vnfortunat at home, in these meetings still vnfortunat: *a me factum est*, is the motto that he gives; all the crosses that doe happen, are but as his corrections, when for want of duty & sincerity in his service, man drawes vpon himself the furie of his anger. I doubt not but the vnhappiness is confest of wch this surely is the cause, for p̃vention wherof in our future labors I shall desire that we may first seeke to make our reconciliation wth God, & according to the p̃sidents & pietye of former meetings humble our selves before him, to wch end my motion shall conclude that ther may be &c̃.

M^r Sp^r I could wishe these things had proceeded from some other, & I had then beene silent; but failing in that desire, & weighing the necessity of the cause, it being for the honor of the K. for the saftie of the kingdome: for the assurance of our frinds, the support of our religion, I could not but against all difficulties resolve as Cicero did in the like, *quemvis mallem suscipere quam me, me autem quam neminem.*"

Eheu! Only a fragment survives of a still greater Speech on religion :—

Folios 52-53. "the like I read of Gratian, (& I beseech y^u well observe it. for in something it comes neerer to the analogie of these times) who, did not onlie make such a signification for the present, but reduc't it to a lawe transmissive to posterity, wch the civilians can testifie from their bookes, wherin both the act, & reason is exprest, wch saies that his rescripts should in nothing be observd when they were contrary to Justice & repugnant to the Lawes, *Quia inverecundâ petentium inhiatione Principes sæpe constringuntur vt non concedenda concedant;* wch expression is soe full, made by soe great a prince, soe great in power & wisdome, confessing the abuses he was subiect to, even to be constraind through the petulance & importunity of his ministers to acts not worthie of himself, that wthout preiudice to their order, naie, in their favor & advantage, the same opinion may be held of the princes that now are, & soe of our deer Sover : whose goodness most does warrant it, & wch is the conclusion I would come to; that if such things have protection by his name, wch in the least pointe are not answearable to his pietie & iustice, we should thinke *inverecunda petentium inhiatione, aut se ignoto,* they are done, either wthout his knowledg or through the misinformation & importunity of some that are about him ; & soe this declaration that is publisht by wch more danger is portended then in all has beene before. ffor in the rest, in all other perticulers of our fears concerning Poperie or Arminianism we are endanger'd by degrees, the evills approching by gradation, one serving as a preparation to another; but in this, like an invndation they breake on vs, soe impetuously & violent, that, leaving art & circumstance, by plaine force they threaten at once, to overwhelme vs, ffor, I beseech y^u marke it, the articles containe the grounds of our religion; the letter of those articles (as the declaration does confess) implies a doubtfull sence; the application of that makes the difference of our adversaries: the interpretation is referrd to the iudgment of the prelates, who have therby the concession of a power to doe anie thing for the maintenance of the truth, wch truth (as I said) being conteined in the articles, & they having double sence vpon wch the differences arise, it is in them to order it wch way they please, & soe, for ought I know, to bring in Poperie or Arminianisme, to wch we must submit. Is it a light thing to have the Canon of Religion rest in the disposition of these men? should the rules & principles of our faith be squard by their affections? I honor both their persons & professions, but give me leave to saie the truth, [what] we have in question, is not mans but Gods, &, god forbid, that man should now be made to iudge it. I remember a character & observation I have seen in a *Diarie* of Edward. 6. that young prince ap^d S^r. R. C. of famous memorie, vnder his owne hand writing of the quality of the B^{ps} of his time, wch saies that *some for sloath, some for age, some for ignorance, some for luxurie, some for poperie, some for all these, were vnfitt for discipline & gover-*

ment. I hope it is not soe wth ours : I make noe application; but we know not what may be heerafter & this reference is intended to the order, not the persons. I speake it not by way of aspersion to our church, I am not such a sonne to seeke the dishonor of my mother (farr be it from me to blemishe that reputation I would vindicate) she has such children in the Hierarchie as may be ffathers to all ages, who shine in virtue, like those faithfull witnesses in heaven, of whom we may vse that elogie wch Seneca did of Cænius, that it be noe preiudice to their meritts *quod nostris temporibus nati sunt.* But they are not all such, I fear : witness those two complaind of in the last remonstrance we exhibited, & y^u know what place they have : witness likewise Mountague, soe newly now preferrd : (I reverence the order though I honor not the man) & others might be namd of the same backe & leven, to whose iudgments, if our religion were committed, it might easilie be discernd what resolution they would give ; wherof, ev'n the procuring of that referenc this manifesto to be made is a perfect demonstration.

This S^r I have given y^u as my apprehension in this pointe, mov'd both by my dutie to y^r service & religion ; & therin, as a symbole of my hart, some thing by way of addition I could grant to the humor of our adversaries even the admission of some ceremonies, those great idolls wch they worship ; that ceremonie I meane wch the Eastern churches vsd of standing at the repetition of the creed ; & not onlie soe to testifie their purpose to maintaine it ; but (as some had it) wth their swords drawne, signifying the constancie and readiness of their resolutions to live & die in that profession : wch resolution I hope we have wth as much constancie assum'd, &, on all occasions shall as faithfullie discharge it, not valuing our lives wher the adventure may be necessarie for the defence of our Soveraigne, for the defence of our Countrie, for the defence of our religion : & this the more earnestlie I deliver for an intimation to our enemies, that they may see from hence what wilbe the issue of their plotts, who by innovation of religion strike at the saftie of the State, & soe seeke to vndermine both Church & King, & Countrie. But, I hope god will direct vs to prevent it, now the danger is discover'd (& to that end my expressions have beene aym'd) wherin to come to a conclusion (all other waies laid by that may be intricat, or confus'd)—Let vs proceed vpon the grounds alreadie laid, that knowne truth we have profest, not admitting questions or disputes, but enquiring who offende against it; whose actions, whose doctrines, whose discourses have beene in preiudice therof; vpon these let vs proceed to examine, to adiudge them : Let their punishments be made exemplarie to others : let these speake the meritts of our cause : they are now actions & not words, that must secure vs against the bouldness & corruption of these times ; for to that disease & sickness, this is the proper medicine. And thus, wth my wonted freedome having presum'd vpon your patienc thus suddainlie to express my self in soe high & great a cause, according to the narrow comprehension of my thoughts, I have given y^u the weake reasons I conceive to shew the danger that's towards vs, &

the prevention it may have, wherin craving wth all humilitie y[r] pardons, I submitt to y[r] grave iudgments & soe leave it to the consideration of the house."

Finally here—we have a Protest drawn up by Eliot and in his handwriting, on the Dissolution of the 3[d] Parliament:—

Fol. 54-55.

"The miserable condition we are in both in matter of rell: & poll: makes me looke wth a tender eye & fearfull apprehensions both on the K. & sub[t]. y[n] know how our rel: is attempted; how Arminianism like a secret pioner vndermines it, & poperie like a strong enemie comes soe on, as it gives, even, a terror to the Lawe; that perticular of the Jesuits concerning their plantation, their new colledg heer amongst vs, wth the other things incident to that, w[ch] our late disquitions have laid open, are such a demonstration & evidence, & soe manifestly doe shew, in a short veiwe, the power & bouldness of that faction, that not to see the danger we are in, were not to know the being that we have; not to confess, not to endeavor to prevent it, were to be conscious & partners of the crime, partners of that evill, w[ch] would conclude vs guiltie, guiltie of the breach & violation of all dutye, our dutie towards god, our dutie to the K., our dutie to our Countrie: nor is this danger only in these men, who are soe active of themselves, soe industrious to evill, as I thinke noe sound man will iudge, that they portend or can be instruments of, our good, I meane these Jesuits, whose virtues are soe knowne that they have beene banisht almost from all States els in christendome & now come for Sanctuarie heer to vs; these men I say, are not the whole cause of the danger we are in, wch yet were not little, though depending meerly vpon them, but it is inlargd by the concurrenc of their fautors, by whose countenance & means they were introduc't, those that have the power & superintendence of lawe, & dare check the magistrat in the execution of all justice: from them likewise comes another line of danger wch points at the center of our hopes, our religion, & from these streames do flowe the causes of our sufferings, our interruptions in this place ; their guilt & fear of punishment cast vs vpon these rocks, having noe confidenc or security in themselves but what they drawe from our trouble & disturbance. there are amongst them some prelates of the churche, wch all ages have had ready for innovation & disturbance, though I fear this time more then anie, the B^p of Winchester & his fellowes doe confirme it, of whom it is apparant what they have done, what practises they have vsd to cast an aspersion on the K., to draw his pietie into question, to give the world ielosie of that. nor are these all, but it extends to others who in like guilt and conscienc of themselves doe ioyne their force wth them to draw his Ma^{te} likewise into ielosie of the parliam^{te}. amongst them I shall not sticke to name that great Lo. Tr$\bar{e}\bar{r}$ & to say that I fear in his person is contracted the verie roote & principle of these evills : I finde him building vpon the ould grounds & foundations wch were laid by the D. of Buckingham his great master : his Counsells I am doubtful begatt that sad issue of the last session, & from that cause, that vnhappie conclusion was contracted. (but for preparation to his reward this note let me give him by the way, that who ever have occasiond such publicke breach in parl[ts], for their privat interests & respects, the felicitye has not lasted to a perpetuitie of that power, but in the end parl[ts] have broke them, the fates in that holdinge correspondencie wth iustice, w[ch] the examples of all ages doe confirme). but to returne to the consideration of our dangers, wherein I deduce not the reason from the affections only of that Lo: of w[ch] their is soe large an indication ; but his relations likewise doe express it, his acts, & operations in their course: does he not strive to make himself & already is become the head of all the papists? have not their priests & Jesuits dailie entercourse wth him? I doubt not but a fewe daies, even in the secrets, will discover it, what plotts & machinations they have laid; vpon w[ch] if y[u] please to spend a little examination, the proofe I am confident wilbe such as will fix it indubitablie vpon him. from whence it may be seene by what influenc & powers are causd our dangers in religion.

In pollicie, wherein like fear is apprehended, the demonstration is as easie, (I can but touch it in respect of the straitness we are in) in that great question of to. and po.* the interest w[ch] is pretended for the K. is but the interest of that person & that vsd as an engine for the removing of our trade, w[ch] cannot but subvert the goverment & K[m]. it was a counsell long since given against vs by Hospi-

---

* Tonnage and poundage.—G.

talis, Chancelor to Charles the 9th of ffrance, that the way to debilitat this state, the way to weaken & infirme it, & soe to make it fitt for conquest & invasion, was not by attempt by outward strength to force it but first to impeach the trade, to hinder or divert it ; to stop it in our hands or to turne it into others, & soe lay waste our walls, these wodden-walls our ships, that both fortifie & enriche vs; wch counsell is now in practise, & that intention brought to act, w^{ch}, though it yett be shadowd by disguise & now stand mask't before vs, I doubt not but a few daies will open & discover, & the purpose wilbe plaine that in this worke is meant our ruine & destruction & to that end strangers are invited to drive our trade, or at least our marchants to trade in strangers bottomes, wch wilbe equally as dangerous; the guilt wherof imprints a fear vpon his conscienc wch makes him misinterpret our proceedings, misrepresent them to his Ma^{te} ; & therefore it is fitt (as true Englishmen) for vs, in discharge of our duties in this case, to shew the affection that we have to the honor & saftie of our Soveraigne ; to shew our affection to religion, & to the rights and interests of the sub^{t}., to declare our purpose to maintaine them, & our resolutions to live & die in their defence: that soe, like our ffathers, we may preserve our selves as freemen, & by that freedome keep abilitie for the supplie & supportation of his Matie, when our services may be needfull : to wch end this paper was conceavd & has' this scope & meaning that

 Wheras by the antient lawes & liberties of England it is the knowne birthright & inheritance of the sub^t. that noe taxe, tollage, or other charge should be levied or imposd but by common consent in par^t. & that the Subsidies of to. & po. are noe waie due or paiable but by a free gifte & speciall Act of par^t. as they were granted to our late Sover. K. J. of blessed memory, by whose death they ceased & determined; & yet notwthstanding they have since beene levied & collected contrary to the said lawes & liberties of the Kingdome & to the great preiudice & violation of the rights & priviledges of par^t., wch said levies & collections have beene formerly heer declared to be an effect of some new Counsells against the antient & settled course of goverment & tending to an innovation therin, & are still an apparant demonstration of the same. The C: therfore now assembled in par^t., being thervnto iustly occasioned for the defence & maintenance of their rights & the said lawes & liberties of the Kingdome doe make this protestation followinge, That if any minister or officer whatsoever shall heerafter counsell or advise the levying or collection of the said subsidies of to. & po. or other charges, contrary to the Lawe; or shall exact, receave or take the same, not being granted or established by speciall Act of Par^t, that they will not only esteeme them (as they were stiled by K. J.) vipers & pests; but also heerby doe declare them to be capitoll enemies of this Kingdome & Commonwealth, & that they will heerafter, as occasion shalbe offred vpon complaint therof in par^t., proceed to inflict vpon them the highest punishm^t wch the lawes appointe to any offender. And if any Marchant or other shall voluntarily yeeld or pay the said subsidies or charges, not granted, as aforesaid, they herby further protest & declare that vpon like complainte therof they will w^thout any favor proceed likewise against them as accessories to the said offences."

From folio 56 to folio 90 are nine batches of 'Precedents' upon a variety of subjects of high historical import, collected by Eliot and personally transcribed by him. On folio 91 are written and pencilled *memoranda* on freedom of debate. On folios 93-4 is the Protest submitted by him in Court at the close of the legal proceedings against him in 1629.

On folios 97-9 are fragments of Speeches that were not spoken. In my judgment they are of rare interest and weight, as thus :—

"As I consider the occasion & this day, I am diversly affected & have such different & contrary apprehensions w^thin me as I hardly know what expression I may give them. the occasion of it self, the accusation of the Att., the bill or information i'th Starch[amb]^r. (to the substanc & materialls wherof it is now expected I should speake by way of answear & apologie, that soe it may bee seene vpon the imputations ther laid, whither I shalbe worthie of a place & favor in your service, & the house neither in point of iustice nor of honor receave a preiudice by the admission) Fol. 96-97.

this occasion (I say) this attempt of proceeding in Star ch^r. this bill or information of the Att^r. caused y^t the bill, casting such dire aspects vpon the servants & members of this house, & wth soe great an influence into the affaires & business of parl^t, like a strange Meteor or constellation does affright me, vnder whose powers I move not wth out fear or wonder. yet this fear I apphend not for my self nor can it be soe narrowly contracted in him that does preferr the consideration of the publick, but for y^r interests I fear, for the respects & interests of this house, for the respects & interests of the K^m, the publicke & common interests of all, for these I confes^s a terror has possest me drawne from the observation of that bill, wch like a prodigie does threaten ruine & destruction. ffor if y^u veiw it in consideration of the Act or ye concommitanc that went wth it, or in the effect & operation that it had, or in the consequence & success it may induce, y^u shall finde it soe violently assaulting the rights & priviledges of this house & soe fully shaking the bases & foundation of the parl^t.

Soe violently assaulting the rights & priviledges of this house, soe cunningly vndermininge the lawes & libertyes of the King, as at once it shakes the bases & foundations of o^r hopes

Fol. 98-99.

the vse & preparation of this day, does render me diversly affected; as I drawe it to the consideration of my selfe & those respects that relate to my poore interests, to my private, it affects me, as a birth day or some time of triumphe & festivity full of all happiness & ioye : but it turning to the publ., as I take this reflection from this house & therin [the] prospect of the king^m. wch heer is represented, it gives me fear & terror; such apprehensions as were held of the Nefasti, wch for their fate & omen the Romans would have blotted from their Calendar. To me (for my pticular) what could be more happy? what more to be desired vpon a charge & accusation laid agst me then to receave it heer, heer to meet my adversary, in this place to be admitted to my answear, wthin these walls to make the defenc & apologie [for] myne innocenc, wher such an integritie is profest as makes y^r Justice in these times even famous to a wonder? this, what ever matter were suggested were I confesse the favor I could wishe for; but on this occasion wch is movd in this individuall accusation, wch speakes only of the affaires & business of parl^t., of the passages & proceedings of this house, the preparations & actions of the members, what could come more properly, what more happily to y^r servant on an accusation of that nature, for matters done in parl^t, heer in parl^t. to answear, wher for the most part I presume the same integrities I shall have both for my witnesses & Judges?"

We now pass into the 'prison' of the Tower; and we find a Speech composed there for that Parliament which came not during the writer's life. It is given (modernized) by Forster (vol. ii. pp. 700-704).

Next, we have the 'Apology for Socrates' (folios 104-130). Then succeed Fragments and Studies of a philosophical treatise (folios 132-176). Thoughts (1), a Fragment, being hints and foreshadowings of the 'Monarchie of

Man' (folio 178): (2), a Fragment on the Government of Israel (folios 180-1): (3), a Fragment on Concord and Discord (folios 182-4): (4), Verses transcribed by Eliot (folio 186). The last is so congruous with Sir John Eliot's 'grave, sweet' piety, that I give it. The initials R. J. represent Richard James, B.D., Sir John's special friend :[1]—

Fol. 186.

"Deer Lord, by whom in darke wombe's shade
I am to fear & wonder made,
Learne me what part I am to bear
on this worlds Stage & theatre.
Miters & Crosiers are not things
that give to my ambition wings:
ffor this I ne're did Mammon woo
nor flatter one great Lord or two,
but wth a simple diett fed
Scarce cloath'd & frinded wth a bed,
But was content in midle ranks
of meaner sorte, to veiw the pranks,
& feats of men, more active, who
are better pleasd in what they doe
then I, who scepticklie scarce dare
of Bear, of Lion, or of Hare,
or the worse race of Malepard.
Lowd speake what I have seene or heard;
yet thrice I have beene hal'd before
our Ephorisms of State, full sore,

---

[1] See my edition of James's Poems, pp. 224/5 (1 vol. 4to. 1880).

against my will : & sure I must
before to tiringe roome of dust
I turne, instruct some scene, I give
my name to storie whils't I Live.
Then, whither on Italian stage,
or Englishe, free or forc't, I rage,
or steale a silent part ; Let bee
Deere Lord my sowles rest ever free.
As of Calanus, Let none saie
trulie of me another daie,
that I, well seene in antique Lore
did other Lords then God adore." "Expl^t
"R. J."

Such are the remarkable things brought together in a single noble folio at Port Eliot. In many ways they have enabled me to supplement the MSS.-proper of these volumes. The Reader will find it rewarding to study the Speeches in the light of Forster's narrative in the 'Biography,' but sooth to say, his perverse fashion (as in all his works, *e.g.* lives of Landor, Dickens, Swift, etc. etc.) of splitting into fragments and *bits* the perfected Speeches and Letters is irritating, and could only be counteracted by giving—as herein—the continuous and complete MSS.

I must add that another (folio) MS. volume at Port Eliot consists of Notes made by Eliot (entirely holograph) of proceedings during the sittings of the First and Second Parliaments of Charles the First. Many appear to have been transcribed from the Clerk's Journals, then, of course, unpublished. In these Notes are also included particulars of interest and importance, as to which there is no other known authentic record. Broadly, we have in these Notes the raw material out of which sprang *Negotium Posterorum*. I regret that I cannot find space for quotations from it. Similarly I must leave untouched a still bulkier (folio) MS. entitled " Collections by and concerning Sir John Eliot, 1622-29, and his Eldest Son, 1646-59." This noble tome contains the material (as before) for both *Negotium Posterorum* 'Tomus Primus' and 'Tomus Secundus.' The following is written on a fly-leaf by Forster:—" Up to p. 271 the contents of this vol. relate to Eliot: after to his son. It contains many interesting Collections of the date of the Parliaments in which Eliot sat, both of James and Charles: some wholly transcribed by him (as in the opening), others largely noted. At pp. 139-162 are the Depositions in the Enquiry against Eliot's conduct in his Vice-admiralty. At pp. 169-70 is the Report of the Committee on the famous Cornwall Election, with marginal notes and additions in the handwriting of Sir Robert Cotton, chairman of the Committee. At pp. 94-96, at p. 168, at pp. 175-84, and at pp. 212-19 are Notes wholly in Eliot's hand relating to matters of Enquiry in Parliament affecting himself, Selden and Suffolk, and other affairs. P. 248 is in Luke's writing. Pp. 233-43 include curious Notes of the Arguments on Eliot's case in the King's Bench, with interlineations and additions by himself." The more's the pity that any such weighty and authentic historical documents should be left in the hazards of MS. only!

I. NOTES AND ILLUSTRATIONS.

I. NOTES AND ILLUSTRATIONS.

⁎ Classical and familiar historical names and events—home and foreign—are not annotated—only such as seemed to require some information for the 'General Reader.' Noticeable words are recorded.—G.

Vol. I.

Page 3, l. 11, '*expiation*' = satisfaction, atonement.

3, l. 16, '*convented*' = summoned—retained in 'convention' still. Now 'convened.'

5, l. 7 (from bottom), '*deprave*' = depreciate. For a historical use of the word see any edition of Dr. Sibbes's Works, *s. v.*

7, l. 11, '*intention*' = fixedness of attention. Cf. p. 15, l. 5 (from bottom), *et alibi*.

8, l. 2, '*delation*.' So p. 27, l. 7, '*delate*.' = accusation—a technical term of the Civil Law.

8, l. 2, '*leven*' = leaven. Cf. Dr. W. A. Wright's 'Word-Book of the English Bible,' *s. n.*

Page 10, l. 7 (from bottom), and p. 13, l. 6, *et alibi*,
'*Rhetra*' = maxim or saying in law.

12, l. 3, '*sad*' = serious, solemn: l. 12, '*inducement*'
= statement of facts alleged by way of
explanation to other material facts. So
'*induce*,' p. 57, l. 4 (from bottom).

12, l. 3 (from bottom), '*ought*' = owed.

13, l. 13, '*fact*' = act, deed.

14, l. 18, '*actual*' = actuated: l. 4 (from bottom),
'*partie*' = person, individual. So p. 16,
l. 10 (from bottom), *et alibi*.

15, l. 6, '*annihil*' = transition-form of 'annihilate':
l. 15, '*interdiccon*' = interdict, arrest of
procedure: l. 16, '*Catastrophe*' = end,
exit: l. 3 (from bottom), '*retentions*'—
in antithesis to 'intentions' = memories
or remembrances. Cf. p. 17, l. 10.

16, l. 17, '*deliction*' = dereliction: or qu. = delict?

17, l. 14, '*confirringe*' = conferring: or qu. confirming?

18, l. 6 (from bottom), '*deductit*' = deduced.

20, l. 4 (from bottom), '*denunciation*' = solemn or
formal declaration.

24, l. 1, '*avoid*' = make void.

26, l. 2 (from bottom), '*affective*' = affects, or ex-
cites emotion.

27, l. 11, '*sociats*' = associates, fellows.

29, l. 3 (from bottom), '*Elege*' = lamentation: or
eulogy?

NOTES AND ILLUSTRATIONS.

Page 35, l. 4, '*Metis.*' Cf. vol. ii. p. 136, ll. 4, 6 : l. 3 (from bottom), '*checker*' = exchequer.

36, l. 8, '*Embrione*' = first rudiments.

37, l. 8, '*censure*' = judgment. General Index, *s. v.*, and for a curious illustration of its changed meaning see vol. i. p. 106, l. 1.

41, l. 6 (from bottom), '*prestigious*' = juggling trickery. Cf. General Index, *s. v.*

43, l. 15, '*desposorio's*' = disposorios, *i. e.* ceremony of betrothal (Spanish): l. 3 (from bottom), '*Chevr'es*' = Chevreuse.

44, l. 18, '*diffidence*' = doubt, hesitation concerning.

46, l. 13, '*poole of Bethesda,*' St. John, c. v. : l. 15, '*prevent*' = anticipate, come before.

47, l. 11 (from bottom), '*nullities*' = nothings, lacking legal force: CREWE. Sergeant Crewe was Sir Thomas Crewe, younger brother of Sir Ranulph Crewe, Lord Chief Justice. He was Speaker of the last Parliament of James I. and first of Charles I. (1625). He died Feb. 1, 1633/4, in his 68th year. His eldest son was created by Charles II. Lord Crewe of Stene.

48, l. 2 (from bottom), '*rubbs*' = hindrances. So in *King John* (iii. 4), ". . . . each little rub out of the path : " and *Richard II.* (iii. 4), " the world is full of *rubbs,*" &c. &c. &c.

52, l. 17, '*Locusts.*' This designation of the Jesuits =

Papists, recalls that Phineas Fletcher gave the name of ' Locustes ' to his remarkable poem—studied by Milton—against the Church of Rome. See my edition of his Poems (4 vols., Fuller Worthies' Library). "The Locustes or Apollyonists:" Latin and English. 1627. 4to.

Page 54, l. 17, '*orbicular*' = form of an orb: l. 21, '*complexion*' = temperament : l. 25, '*artificiallie*' = with art, skilfully: l. 28, '*commensuration*' = measure or measurement.

59, l. 20, '*resent*' = resentment, either in transition-form or written contractedly : l. 2, '*pretended*'—*not* as implying hypocritical acceptance.

60, l. 9 (from bottom), '*preachers were design'd*' [= designated] for both. No capable historical student will regret examination of the large collections of the ' public ' and 'fast' Sermons of the great Puritan Preachers. It is a mystery to me that modern Historians do not more resort to these. They are packed with the thoughts that were in the air and the emotion that made many hearts beat slow or fast; while there are universally personal and local allusions that are of rarest interest as manners-painting.

Page 61, SIR JOHN SAVILL or Savile—of Howley, Yorkshire. He was created Baron Savile of Pontefract, 21 July, 1628, and died in 1630. His son was created Earl of Sussex, which title became extinct in 1671.

62, l. 5 (from bottom), '*induc'd*' = adduced. See under 'inducement' on p. 12, l. 12.

64, l. 13, '*contestation*' = contest, debate : l. 6, '*Briarius*,' = Briareus—Eliot spelled his Latin much as he did his English.

77, SIR ROBERT PHELIPS, Kt.—M.P. for Somersetshire in 1st and 2nd Parliaments of Charles I. He was of the family of Phelips of Montacute, co. Somerset, still there. He was eldest son of Sir Edward Phelips, Speaker of the House of Commons. Died 1638. It is surely lamentable that no worthy Memoir of this preeminent man has been furnished.

81, l. 13, '*winter towness.*' *Sic*, but=Winterton Ness: SIR SYMON HARVIE—knighted at Theobalds Oct. 3, 1623, being then Remembrancer of the King's Household. He was buried at Isleworth, Middlesex, Dec. 4, 1628. Villiers wanted to marry his daughter Christophe, whilst Sir Simon was Lord Mayor. So Mr. Gardiner informs me. *Ibid.*, SIR JOHN MILDRAM = Sir John Meldrum. See Col. Chester's

"Westminster Abbey Registers" (p. 13), and note. He was a courtier who got a grant of tolls for a lighthouse at Wintertonness, on which there was much to-do in the Parliament of 1621. See Debates.

Page 83, l. 12, '*Pennie.*' *Sic*, but = Binnie.

87, l. 8, '*intreatment*' = treatment. All such prefixing of 'in,' &c. &c., to be noted, in relation to Shakespeare and the *crux* of the Sonnet-deduction.

89, l. 20, '*obsolved.*' *Sic*, but = absolved.

94, SIR FRANCIS SEYMOUR—younger son of Edward Lord Beauchamp. He was created Feb. 19, 1640-1, Baron Seymour of Trowbridge. He died July 12, 1664, and was buried at Bedwin, Wilts. His grandson Charles, became sixth Duke of Somerset, known as the "Proud Duke."

95, l. 21, '*venie*' = venue—in law, a neighbourhood or place.

96, l. 10, '*practises*' = malpractice or evil arts. So p. 133, l. 2.

97, l. 4 (from bottom), '*protraction*' = drawing out, delay.

104, l. 9, '*sent'iarum*' = sen*t*entiarum: SIR WILLIAM COPE—2nd Bart. of Brewerne, co. Oxon. —son of Sir Anthony Cope, 1st Bart.— sometime M.P. for Banbury, and after-

NOTES AND ILLUSTRATIONS. 161

wards for the county of Oxford. He died Aug. 2, 1637, aged 60.

Page 109, l. 6, '*cunctation*' = delay.

110, l. 10, '*privado's*' = secret friend (in a bad sense): SIR HUMPHREY MAY. See Col. Chester's "Westminster Abbey Registers" (p. 129), and note.

113, SIR JOHN COKE—of Melbourne, co. Derby, 2nd son of Richard Coke of Trusley—sometime Secretary of the Navy, afterwards Master of the Requests and Secretary of State—M.P. for Cambridge in 1st Parliament of Charles I. He continued in public life till 1639, when he retired to Melbourne, where he died Sept. 8, 1644, in his 82nd year.

116, l. 3 (from bottom), '*brandle*' = brangle, *i. e.* wrangle.

117, SIR THOMAS GRANTHAM—M.P. for Lincoln city in the first two Parliaments of Charles I.—not historically famous.

121, l. 5, '*exinanition*' = emptying.

130, l. 19, '*covenable*' = fit, suitable. So 'unconvenable,' p. 91, l. 6 : l. 21, '*retribucons*' = repayments, rewards.

133, l. 9 (from bottom), '*preiudicate*' = prejudged.

137, l. 6, '*perspective*' = glass, *e. g.* telescope, &c. : l. 7, '*derived*' = communicated : l. 13, '*representive*' = representative.

Page 161, l. 8, '*minion*' = favourite—now deteriorated into 'parasite,' and worse.
169, l. 17, '*involution*' = entanglement.

Vol. II.

3, l. 3, '*infestuous*' = mischievous.
4, l. 1, '*strengths*' = strongholds.
6, EARL OF NOTTINGHAM—Charles Howard, who succeeded his father as 2nd earl of Nottingham, Dec. 14, 1624—died Oct. 3, 1642. He led against the Armada.
9, l. 7, '*elogie*' = lament.
11, SIR HENRY MARTEN—the distinguished advocate and judge, successively of the Admiralty, Prerogative Court, and the Arches. He died Sept. 26, 1641. He was hung as one of the Regicides.
12, EARL OF CARLISLE—James Hay, the well-known favourite of James I., who created him Earl of Carlisle in 1622. Charles I. also made him 1st gentleman of his bedchamber. He died April 25, 1636, and the title became extinct on the death of his son in 1660: *ibid.*, EARL OF HOLLAND—Sir Henry Rich, K.B. (2nd son of Robert, 1st earl of Warwick)—captain of the king's guard, was created Baron Kensington in 1622, and Earl of Holland,

co. Lincoln, Sept. 24, 1624. By his wife he became possessor of the famous 'Holland House' in Kensington. For an attempt to rescue Charles I., when prisoner in the Isle of Wight, he was committed to the Tower, and eventually executed March 9, 1649.

Page 15, l. 11, '*voge*' = going, *i.e.* general opinion.

21, l. 8, '*postill*' = gloss or marginal note.

25, l. 9, '*foulkers*' = famous money-lenders.

36, l. 3, '*exhaust*' = exhausted : l. 4, '*checker*' = exchequer, as before : l. 9 (from bottom) : SIR RICHARD WESTON—of Roxwell, Essex—ambassador abroad in reign of James I., and afterwards Chancellor of the Exchequer. He was created Baron Weston April 13, 1628, and Earl of Scotland Feb. 17, 1633 : died March 13, 1634.

42, l. 8 (from bottom), '*removent*' . . . '*promovent*' = removing, promoting : CRANFIELD— Lionel Cranfield, Earl of Middlesex. See Col. Chester's "Westminster Abbey Registers" (p. 139) for his burial, and note.

43, l. 1, '*largess*' = bounty.

45, *King's Solicitor.* = Solicitor General. He was Sir Robert Heath. See Forster and Gardiner, as before *frequenter*.

Page 48, l. 6, '*touch*' = stroke.
,, l. 14, '*contestation*' = contest, debate, as before.
49, l. 8, '*atonement*' = making-at-one, reconciliation : l. 18, '*partie*' = person, individual, as before : l. 26, '*increpation*' = chiding. So p. 81, l. 6 (from bottom).
51, WILLIAM CLARKE, Esq., was M.P. for Agmondesham, Bucks, in 2nd Parliament of Charles I. summoned to meet in Feb., 1625/6—not historically known.
68, l. 14, '*budding*' = beginning—a favourite word contemporarily.
75, l. 14, '*swasorie*' = persuasion.
77, l. 25, '*thrasonicall*' = bragging.
81, l. 18, '*sophistries*' = fallacious reasoning : *ib.* '*sophisters*' = sophists—not as in technical university terms.
84, SIR ROBERT MANSELL—younger brother of Thomas Mansel, 1st baronet of Margam, ancestor of the Lords Mansell of Margam. He was knighted for his valour at the capture of Calais in 1596, and subsequently became rear-admiral of England. He was M.P. for Glamorganshire in the 1st Parliament of Charles I. He died at a great age in 1652.
87, BISHOP WICKHAM, the celebrated founder of New College, Oxford : died 1404.

NOTES AND ILLUSTRATIONS.

Page 90, l. 17, '*vasted*' = wasted—used much as 'vaded' and 'faded.'
,, JOHN GLANVILLE, Esq.—of Tavistock—Recorder of Plymouth, was M.P. for Plymouth in 2nd Parliament of Charles I. as well as in the 1st. He became Speaker of the House of Commons in 1640, and was knighted Aug. 7, 1641. He died Oct. 2, 1661, and was buried at Broad Hinton, Wilts.
97, LORD CHICHESTER—Edward, 3rd son of Sir John Chichester, of Raleigh, co. Devon, was created, April 1, 1625, Baron and Viscount Chichester. He died in 1648—ancestor of first Earl of Donegal.
98, l. 4, '*manifer*' = manifest : l. 18, '*Colophon*' = conclusion.
116, l. 8, '*caulupon*' = call upon? (unintelligible.)
127, l. 18, '*tinners*' = lessors of the tin-mines.
140, l. 9, '*elogie*' = eulogy.
143, l. 5, '*fautors*' = favourers, patrons.

II. GENERAL INDEX OF NAMES AND THINGS.

II. GENERAL INDEX OF NAMES AND THINGS.

⁎ Under 'Speech,' 'Parliament,' and the like, will be found full statements of which details are separately given in this Index. So also under prominent names, *e.g.* Charles, Buckingham, Eliot, the principal events, &c.

A.

BSURDITIE, in reason, i. 16.
 Accusacon, Socrates did not answear, i. 5 : made against him, i. 7.
 Accusers, i. 5, 58.
Achan, ii. 136.
Actions, substance of, i. 8 : not discourse, i. 44.
Adjornment, of Parliament, i. 61, 62, 63, 121, 122 : only by House of Commons itself, 124.
Admiracon, i. 4.
Admiralty, abuses in, ii. 44.
Adventurers, merchant, i. 82.
Aer, will vindicate Socrates, i. 6.

GENERAL INDEX.

Affect, affected, i. 78, 79, 96.
Affections, i. 6.
Affective, i. 26.
Afflictions, of the time, ii. 46.
Agitations, in Parliament, i. 36.
Ajax, i. 8.
Alehouses, restraint of, i. 126.
Alexander the Great, ii. 118.
Algiers, ii. 124.
Alienation, license of, i. 126.
Allegations, i. 10.
Alnage, i. 83.
Ambassadors, i. 43, 44, 75, 85: gratification to, ii. 11.
Ancestors, ii. 113.
Anderson, a great lawyer, ii. 121.
Andrians, i. 157.
Anian, Dr., i. 82: forbidden to preach, ii. 15, 16. See Wood's Ath. Oxon. s. n.
Annihil, i. 15.
Answear, Socrates did not, i. 5, 26: particular, i. 6: to petition of religion, ii. 57 onward. See vol. i. 84 onward.
Antiquitie, i. 8.
Anytus, i. 5, 7, 14.
Apologie for Socrates=a Vindication of Sir John Eliot by himself, i. 1-30: difficulty of, i. 5.
Apollo, i. 35, 42.
Apothecaries, patent of, i. 81.
Apparant, i. 88.

Architophles, i. 71.
Argument, libertie of, i. 7.
Arguments, needed, i. 6.
Argus, i. 64 : ii. 55.
Arminians, i. 106, 107 : ii. 102, 137.
Army, leader of, i. 115.
Arrears, ii. 72.
Arrest, noe legal, i. 10, 53, 58.
Arrowes, more, ii. 55.
Articles, of Church of England, i. 106.
Aspersions, scandalous, i. 3.
Assemblie, sacred, i. 3.
Assent, Commission of, i. 122.
Assumption, of the judges, i. 28.
Athenians, pietie and justice of, example of, i. 3 : pardon sought from, i. 4 : wisdomes of, i. 7 : pardon again asked, i. 7 : patience of, i. 7 : birthright of, i. 11.
Athens (= England), prosperity of, i. 12, 21, 26.
Atlas, i. 4.
Attensions, i. 7.
Augustine, St., i. 58.
Authoritie, not submitting to, i. 5, 19 : reasons and, i. 8 : of Law, i. 21.
Avoid, i. 24, 89.
Ayd, enlargement of, i. 75.
Aydes, new, i. 62.

B.

Banburie, i. 104 : new election for, i. 105.
Basset, M.P., i. 105.
Be, not seeme, i. 25.
Beginnings, i. 66.
Beecher, i. 117.
Bees, ii. 121.
Bertius, i. 106.
Bethesda, i. 46.
Betrayinge, of liberty, i. 5.
Bible, quoted, i. 48, 49.
Bichrie, sons of, i. 52, 58.
Bill, for two Subsidies, i. 92.
  „   for Tonnage and Poundage, i. 93.
Binnie [misprinted 'Pennie'], i. 83.
Birthright, i. 9.
Bishops, to be careful, i. 87.
Blame-after, i. 9.
Body, well-composed, i. 54.
Bohemia, queen of, ii. 25.
Books of Mountagu, i. 79, 80, 106 : Popish and seditious, i. 81, 86.
Bottoms, English, i. 83.
Bouldnesse, i. 4.
Bracton, ii. 40.
Brandle, i. 116.
Breaches, occasions of, i. 131-2.

Breda, i. 116.
Briareus, i. 64.
British and Irish, ii. 59.
Buckingham, duke of, interposes, i. 110: interview with Eliot, i. 111-12 : in bed with 'Dutchess,' i. 111 : most blameable, i. 118 : character of, i. 118-19 : influence of, i. 119 : message of king by, ii. 11: present at Oxford, ii. 18 : singled out, ii. 31, 42 : defended by Clarke, ii. 51: ill-advised, ii. 54: modification of acts, ii. 54, 55: celebrated speech of, on Petition for Religion, ii. 56 onward: self-vindication, ii. 62 : letters of the king to, ii. 64: associates in counsell, ii. 64 : audacity of, ii. 76: faultie, ii. 94, 106, 107, 108 : designs of, ii. 124: speech of Eliot after B.'s assassination, ii. 134: master of king, ii. 143, *et passim*.
Buckler, of State, i. 8.
Buildings, i. 82.
Bul-baitings, i. 126.
Burgo, H. de, i. 161.
Business, urgent in Parliament, i. 46.

C.

Cæsar, i. 46.
Cales, expedition to, i. 158 : ii. 123.
Canopie, of State, i. 8.
Canterburie, i. 43.
     ,,   Archbishop of, i. 70, 78 : censured, i. 79.
'Captives,' English, by Turks, ii. 3, 4.

Carlile, earl of, ii. 12. See *Notes and Illustrations*.
Cataline, i. 104.
Catastrophe, i. 15.
Catechise, i. 86.
Catholic Church, ambition of, i. 169-170.
Catholicon, a, i. 66.
Catholike League, i. 117.
Cause, of Socrates, i. 7.
Cecill, Sir Edward, ii. 97, 98, 107.
Cercumstance, i. 7.
Certioraries, i. 73.
Censure, i. 37, 45, 59, 63, 106, 133.
Chancellor of the Dutchies, ii. 26.
Change, welcome *per se*, i. 42.
Changing names, by Jesuits, i. 73.
Chaplaines, Bishops', i. 87.
Character, a rare, i. 3.
Charges, against Socrates, i. 6.
Charges and expenditures of king, ii. 20, 37.
Charles I., accession of, hopes on, i. 41, 42 : early character, i. 41, 42 : recreations, i. 42 : Parliament called by, i. 43 : at Canterburie, i. 43 : marriage of, i. 43 : speech on opening Parliament, i. 44 : disabilitie of speech, i. 44 : father's daies, i. 44 : motto of, i. 47 ; good service of, while prince, i. 48 : undoubted heir, i. 49 : 'great expectations' of, i. 49 : his proud inheritance, i. 50 : dying advice of father, i. 50 : safe return from Spain, i. 50, 51 : love of Parliaments, i. 56 : lineage, i. 56 : religious, i. 57 : good influence, i. 66 : personal religion,

GENERAL INDEX. 175

i. 67 : 'strict' life, i. 67 : bred in Parliaments, i. 67 : confidence shewn towards, i. 68 : domestic charges, i. 75 : funeral of father, i. 75 : message from the king, i. 92 : at Hampton Court, i. 92 : demands 'Supply' through Buckingham, i. 114 : expenditures, i. 114 : 'confederacies,' i. 115 : appeals of the king, i. 116 : answer real, not verbal, i. 122-3 : protects Mountagu, ii. 14 : speech at Oxford, ii. 17 : condition, ii. 37 : married the person, not the religion of his queen, ii. 60 : new message of, ii. 79 : great debts of, ii. 88 onward : Eliot's confidence in, i. 133, *et passim.*

Charter, great, i. 48.
Checker, i. 35.
Chevr'es=Chevreuse, i. 43.
Chichester, Lord, ii. 97. See *Notes and Illustrations.*
Child, a, i. 18.
Christ College, Oxford, ii. 16.
Church, absence from, fines for, i. 90.
Cicero, i. 77, 102, 104, 159 : ii. 116, 122, 132, 137.
Claimes and challenges, i. 9, 10.
Clarke, Mr., ii. 51 : at bar, ii. 52. See *Notes and Illustrations.*
Clergie, subsidies granted by, i. 126.
Cloth, trade of, i. 82 : various, i. 82 : duties on, i. 82-3.
Cloth-workers, i. 83.
Coales, i. 81.
Cœnus, ii. 140.
Cognisance, i. 11.
Coke, Sir Edward, ii. 39, 92.

Coke, Sir John, i., 113 : misconduct of, ii. 6, 7 : dictator, 18 : speech for king, ii. 55, 67. See *Notes and Illustrations*.
Commenda's, i. 87.
Commission, i. 162 : ii. 104.
Commissioners of the Navy, turned to evil, ii. 6.
Commitment, i. 64.
Committee of Privileges, i. 60, 61.
„ grand, of Greivances, i. 63.
„ of Religion, i. 65.
„ naming of, i. 63, 64 : three, i. 63, 64.
„ of House of Commons, i. 93 : ii. 56.
Commons, House of, first acts of, i. 60 : described, i. 93 : dispersal of, i. 125.
Communion ('Lord's Supper'), i. 60.
Complaint, of Socrates i. 7 : translating of, i. 8.
'Complexion,' i. 54.
Concealments, patent of, i. 80.
Conclave, i. 22.
Concourse, and assemblie, i. 7.
Concurringe, of judges, i. 11.
Conference of two Houses, i. 70.
Confirring = confirminge, i. 17.
Conforming, i. 21, 89.
Conscience, i. 9, 13, 15, 21, 25.
Consequences, i. 22.
Constellation, ominous, i. 106.
Construction, favorable, i. 58.
Consulto, ii. 108.

Contempt, of justice, i. 5, 19, 21, 23.
Convented, i. 3.
Conway, Lord, ii. 17, 55.
Cope, Sir William, case of, i. 104, 105. See *Notes and Illustrations.*
Cornwall, leases in Duchy of, i. 125 : state of, ii. 3, 4, 5.
Corruption, of judges, i. 5.
Cotton, Sir Robert, i. 129.
Counsell, to be held, ii. 50 : of War, ii. 64, 65.
Counterpoise and weight, i. 4.
Country, gentleman, i. 75.
Court, no lesser, i. 8 : papists forbidden, i. 88.
Courtiers, i. 75, 78, 118; ii. 26, 48, 84, 91.
Cousenage, i. 73.
Cranfeild, ii. 42. See *Notes and Illustrations.*
Crassus, i. 104.
Credit, of England, ii. 25, 37.
Crew, Crewe, Speaker, i. 47 : character of, i. 47, 140. See *Notes and Illustrations.*
Crimes, i. 5.
Cunctation, i. 109.
Cunninge, i. 5.
Currance, i. 84.
Custome, ancient, i. 11 : customes, i. 83.

D.

Dangers, i. 22.
David, i. 50, 62.

Debts, crown, of Elizabeth and James, ii. 85.
Deductit, i. 18.
Defection, i. 16, 19.
Defence, of Socrates, i. 3, 6.
Delation, i. 8, 27.
Deliberacon, i. 12.
Denmarke, i. 75 : ii. 17, 27, 61, 72, 77.
Deprave, i. 5.
Desertion, of innocence, i. 5.
Desposorio's, i. 43.
Detraction, i. 5.
Devolve, i. 30.
Devonshire, earl of, ii. 27, 28.
Diffidence, i. 44.
Dilemma, i. 16.
Disarming, of recusants, i. 89.
Discipline, of Universities, i. 86.
Discovery, Socrates must not make, i. 13, 14, 22.
Discreation, i. 17, 99.
Disorders, origin of, i. 141.
Dissimulation, i. 36.
Dissolution, of Parliament, ii. 104, 105, 106, 132-7.
Divine, lawyer, i. 59 : divines, i. 107.
Dolphine, ii. 93.
Dorsetshire, Jesuits in, ii. 49.
Dort, i. 79, 106.
Dover, i. 115 : troops at, ii. 27.
Duncombe's case, i. 139-40.
Dunkerks, ii. 93.

Duty, i. 21.
'Dyet,' called, ii. 19, 21.

E.

Ear, i. 6.
East Land Merchants, a Company for trading in the Baltic, i. 84.
Edward I., i. 33, 144.
  „   II., i. 33.
  „   III., i. 33; ii. 39, 50.
  „   IV., i. 34.
  „   VI., i. 34, 94 : Diary of, ii. 139.
Edward's, St., shrine, ii. 89.
Education, of youth, i. 86.
Egypt, i. 51, 58.
Election, for Yorkshire, i. 95 : delays, i. 98-101 : why so fully related, i. 103.
Elege, i. 29.
Eliot, Sir John, pride in defending Socrates, i. 3, 4 : imperfections acknowledged, i. 7 : in prison, pathetic application to himself, i. 29, 30 : speech on religion, i. 70-73 : *ibid.* against Wentworth, i. 101-2 : May appeals to him to meet Buckingham, i. 111 : speech in 1623/4, i. 124-139 : at Oxford, i. 141-8 : on Supply, i. 148 onward : i. 156 onward : of religion and liberty, i. 164 onward : of a Fund, i. 171-3 : speech at Oxford, ii. 9-10 : disbarred, ii. 17 : speech on Supply, ii. 81 onward : on precedents, ii. 85 onward : of Supply, ii.

112-18 : of liberty of person, ii. 119-23 : of miscarriages of reign, ii. 123-5 : of Mohun, ii. 125-30, 130-4 : after death of Buckingham, ii. 133 onward : in the Tower, ii. 149.
Eliot, Port, MSS. at, i. 129 : ii. 152, *et passim*.
Elizabeth, Q., splendid praise, i. 34 : affection for Parliaments, i. 35 : memories of, i. 37, 69, 76, 77, 94, 141, 142, 163 : ii. 25, 26, *et passim*.
Eloquence, of Socrates, i. 6.
'Enapt,' i. 68.
End, and issue, i. 46.
Endimion, i. 42.
Enemies, i. 3, 5.
Engagement, none but by act, ii. 44 : pressed, ii. 47.
England, New, plantation of, i. 80.
England, under Elizabeth, i. 35, 77 : condition of later, i. 130-3 : ii. 3-4, 5, 51, 97.
England's Parliament, i. 33.
    „   West Parts, ii. 3.
Englishman, a proud name, i. 33 : better fighters than treaty-makers, ii. 11.
Enterludes, i. 126.
'Eolus,' i. 110.
Equalls, i. 18.
'Errors,' i. 65 : declaration of, ii. 72 onward.
Estate, King's, ii. 68.
Europe, i. 46.
Evils, national, ii. 42.
Examinacon, i. 22.

Example and examples, i. 3, 7, 29.
Expiation, i. 3.
Expression, defect of, i. 7.
Extempore speaking, best liked in House of Commons, i. 78.
Exuberance, i. 77.

F.

Fact, i. 13, 14, 22, 24, 28, 63.
Factions, fractions, i. 72, 132.
Faith, justifying, i. 107.
Fame, of the king, i. 46.
Fasting, i. 60, 90: reply of king on, i. 74: of, 172: held, i. 74: day appointed, ii. 16.
ffleta, i. 108.
ffoulkers, ii. 25.
Fidelitie, to king, i. 44.
Fifteenths, i. 46, 62, 76, 115, 153.
Fines, of recusants, i. 90.
Fleet, idle, ii. 4: to go forth, ii. 17: dancing a pavine, ii. 44: to go out, ii. 53, 54, 55, 61: costly undertaking, ii. 66-67.
Flies, of Court, i. 34.
Forfeitures, i. 73.
Forme, inward, i. 8.
Foro iudicij, in foro conscientiæ, i. 9.
Forster, John, i. 129, 130, 139, 140: ii. 149, 151, 152 *et passim*.

GENERAL INDEX.

Fragments, of unspoken speeches, ii. 147-9.
France, in combustion, ii. 19.
Frauds, ii. 42.
Freedom, in debate, *memoranda* on, ii. 147.
Freeholders, certificate of, i. 96.
Free speech, i. 53, 58.
French, i. 43, 44, 77 : ships assigned to, ii. 7.

G.

Game, and plaie of favorits, ii. 77.
Gascoyne, Gascoine, i. 146 : ii. 89.
Gate, in Yorkshire election, i. 97, 100.
Gaunt, duke of, ii. 15.
Gaveston, ii. 88.
Genius, of Socrates, i. 4.
Genoa, ii. 27.
Germans, ii. 17, 19, 27, 61.
Giving, and withholding, argued out, ii. 82, 83.
Glanvile, ii. 92, 105. See *Notes and Illustrations*.
Gods, metaphors from heathen, ii. 128, 129.
Gondamar, a juggling jacke, i. 142 : ii. 86.
Gould-wire drawers, i. 80.
Government, i. 8.
Grace, of Socrates, i. 6.
Grantham, Sir Thomas, i. 117. See *Notes and Illustrations*.
Grants, to recusants, i. 89.
Gratian, ii. 138.

Gravitie, of House of Commons, ii. 52.
Greivance, of Socrates, i. 7 : grand committee of, i. 63 : opposition to, i. 65 : divers grounds, i. 65 : answer to, i. 80 : addition to, ii. 49.
Grevile, Sir Foulk, i. 113, 114.
Gubertus, i. 54.
Guiltie, Socrates because not, i. 5.

H.

Hannibal, i. 104.
Happiness, common, i. 44.
Harley, Sir Simon, ii. 14 (see s. n. Harvie).
Harvie, Sir Symon, i. 81 : ii. 42.
Head, the, i. 8.
'Heat,' declined, i. 68.
Heathens, put religion first, i. 71.
Hector, i. 8.
Heighten, i. 5.
Henry III., i. 33, 38, 135, 146 : ii. 89 *et passim.*
„ IV., i. 13, 15, 21, 34 *et passim.*
„ V., i. 33: ii. 102.
„ VI., i. 11, 12, 18, 33, 94, 120, 123 : ii. 89 *et passim.*
„ VII., i. 34, 94 *et passim.*
„ VIII., i. 13, 21, 34, 94.
Hercules, i. 4.
Hezekiah, i. 49.
Hierarchie, unchristian, i. 52.

Holland, earl of, ii. 12. See *Notes and Illustrations*.
Hollanders, i. 35.
Homer, i. 45.
Honors, set to sale, ii. 87.
Hope, good, i. 109, 110.
Hospitalis, ii. 144.
House of Commons, i. 12.
Household, royal, ii. 41, 42.
Humiliation, day of, i. 60: occasion of, i. 60.

I.

Immunities, i. 10, 15, 52.
Impeachment, i. 11.
Impositions, i. 69, 70, 94: limitation of, i. 94: consent refused for, i. 95: multiplied, i. 143: inquired into, ii. 50, 87 *et passim*. See Gardiner's History under "Impositions" on currants, tobacco, &c., and note to Buckingham and Charles I., 32.
Impossibilities, not commanded, i. 16.
Imprisonment of members, i. 12.
Inducement, i. 12, 15.
Infection, of 'sowles,' i. 65.
Infelicities, of England, under James I., i. 42, 69.
Inferiors, i. 18, 19.
Informers, i. 5, 8, 13, 14.
Innocence, of Socrates, i. 3: desertion of, i. 5, 23, 25: 'his innocence' a phrase, i. 6, 24, 26.
Innovations, i. 166.

GENERAL INDEX.

Insolencies, of papists, i. 90.
Integritie, unmatcht, i. 3.
Intelligence, given, i. 13.
Intention, i. 7, 9.
Interdiccon, i. 15.
Interest, public, i. 25.
Intervenients, i. 99.
Interview, of Eliot with Buckingham, i. 111-13.
Ireland, i. 90, 91, 107, 114 : ii. 14, 20, 28, 43, 46, 60, 62.

J.

Jailes, custody of, i. 8.
James I., i. 11 ('occasion of some fear') : death of, i. 41, 49 : long orations of, i. 45 : engagements to, i. 45 : last parliament of, i. 48, 55 : complaints to, i. 65, 66 : petitions to, i. 74 : infortunities of, i. 77 : supported Mountagu, i. 79 : laws, i. 94 : warrant of, i. 105 : 'if Mountagu a Papist so he,' i. 105 : servants of, i. 141, 142 : case of interposition, ii. 15 : deceived in Spain, ii. 32 : debts of, ii. 72 : bad times of, ii. 114 *et passim*.
James, Richard, B.D., ii. 150-151.
Jesuits, i. 52, 65, 73 : contrivances of, i. 73 : non-execution of laws against, i. 85 : departure of, i. 88 : pardon of, i. 167, 169 : ii. 8 : power to, ii. 87 : pardons, ii. 102.
Joel, i. 70.
Jotham, i. 50.

Judas, i. 108.
Judges, corruption of, i. 5: ordinary, i. 9: resolucon of, i. 11, 12, 14: enlarging authority of, i. 27, 28.
Judgment, a, not greater than a process, i. 20.
Jupiter, ii. 123.
Jurisdicon, i. 8, 11, 13, 15, 22, 27.
Justice, i. 3: contempt of, i. 5, 9, 19, 23: embodied, i. 7, 17: defined, i. 24, 25.

K.

King, three necessaries for a, ii. 41.
„ dignity of, i. 137.
„ no private knowledge of legislation, ii. 14.
Kings, for and against Parliaments, i. 33-4, 35, 36: various great, i. 94.
Kingsale (=Kinsale), ii. 28.
Knowledge, 'solitarie,' i. 67.

L.

Lands, royal, resumed, i. 161.
Laro, de Count, ii. 83.
Latimer, Lord, ii. 15.
Law, defection from the, i. 5, 16, 19: equivalent of, i. 10: senate makes, i. 12: certain, i. 21: common, i. 57: to be executed, i. 89.
Laws, statutes, i. 9, 12, 18: sufficient and full, i. 73: non-execution of, i. 73.

Lawyers, i. 10, 29, 59 : ii. 22.
Leagues, ii. 37 : Spanish, ii. 41.
Learning, from others, i. 131.
'Leaves fruitful' (= prerogatives), i. 48, 55.
'Lectures' ridiculed, i. 107.
'Lenitie' to Mountagu, i. 79.
Lepidus, ii. 96.
Letters, obtained, i. 74.
Levant, merchants, i. 83.
Level, of reason, i. 7.
Leven, i. 8, 167.
Lewis, St., ii. 10.
Liberties, betraying of, i. 5 : sanctuary of, i. 8 : franchise and, i. 11, 12, 14, 16, 26, 167-8 *et passim*: England, last 'free' monarchy, ii. 82-3. (See under 'Religion.')
Licenses, called breifes, i. 81.
Lincoln, Bp. of, i. 45. (See under 'Williams.')
Lives, question for, i. 10.
Livings, unfurnished, i. 87.
Livy, i. 104.
Locusts, i. 52.
London, resort of recusants to, i. 90 : seat of Parliament, i. 124.
Lords, numbers doubled of Commons' deputations, i. 91 ; commission on adjournment, i. 121 : interpretation belongs not to, ii. 24.
Low Countries, i. 77 : ii. 19, 20.
Lucius, i. 52.

Lyco, i. 5, 8, 14.
Lying, no, i. 24.

M.

Machiavel, ii. 123.
Malice, i. 5.
Mallet, a lawyer, ii. 75.
'Manner,' i. 46.
Mansell, Sir Robert, ii. 84, 93, 95, 97. See *Notes and Illustrations*.
Mansfelt, Count, i. 45, 75, 76, 114, 115: ii. 20, 21, 27, 124 *et passim*.
Marcellus, ii. 126, 127.
Marchant adventurers, i. 82.
Mars, i. 35, 42.
Marten, Sir Henry, ii. 11: character of, ii. 12, 13, 95. See *Notes and Illustrations*.
Mary, queen, i. 34, 94.
Maxim. Tirr., i. 3.
May, Sir Humphrey, i. 110. See *Notes and Illustrations*.
Mayne, dutchy of, loss of, ii. 87.
'Mediating interest' of Charles I., i. 66.
Melitus, i. 5, 7, 9, 14, 23.
Members, ill, i. 8.
Men, great, dependence on, i. 73.
Merchants, 'spoiled' of Turks, ii. 4.
Meros, i. 51, 58.
Message, new and urgent of the king, ii. 79, 80.

Meteor, ii. 148.
Metis, i. 35 ; ii. 136.
Middlesex, Lord, i. 140.
Milan, ii. 21.
Mildram, Sir John, i. 81. See *Notes and Illustrations.*
Minerva, i. 35.
Minions, ii. 21.
Ministers, silenced, i. 87.
Miscarriages, of the reign, ii. 123-125.
Miserie, i. 131.
Moab, i. 71.
Mohun, speech on, ii. 125-30, 130-4.
Monies, to be wanted foreseen, ii. 67.
Monopolies, i. 69, 70.
Montagu, proceedings with, i. 78, 79 ; books of, i. 79 : ii. 15 : in attendance, i. 105, 106, 107 : offences of, i. 106, 107 : charges against, i. 108 : to be imprisoned, i. 108 ; called in, i. 109 : protected, i. 125 : cause resumed, ii. 13 : not forthcoming, ii. 13 : left to punishment, ii. 54.
Moors, wars against, ii. 83.
Mouth too narrow, i. 7 : children of the, i. 78.
MSS. at Port Eliot, ii. 151-2.
Mulct, i. 16, 73.
Multiplicitie of offices in no man, ii. 42, 43.
Multum in parvo, i. 45.

N.

Naples, ii. 103.
Naunton, Sir Robert, character of and speech, ii. 80.
Navy, i. 45, 114 : ii. 6.
'Necessarie' things, i. 68.
Necessitie, three orders of, ii. 40.
Nefasti, ii. 149.
Neglect, of Socrates, i. 5, 24.
Negotium Posterorum, tom. 2, lib. i., i. 31-126 : design of, i. 36-7 : tom. sec. lib. 2, ii. 1-10, and onward.
Nero, ii. 12.
New castell coales, i. 81.
New wares, i. 117 : ii. 118.
Non-attendance at House of Commons, i. 93.
Non-residence, i. 87.
North, the, i. 62, 96.
Notion, i. 11.
Nottingham, earl of, ii. 6. See *Notes and Illustrations*.
Nullities, i. 47.

O.

Obedience, i. 55.
Object, i. 4, 7, 15.
Objections, particular, i. 6.
Obligaccon, i. 4.
Obsolved, i. 89.
Occasion, new, i. 28.

Oders, i. 10.
Offence, i. 5.
Olivero, Count, = Olivares, ii. 69, 70, 77. See *Notes and Illustrations*.
Ominous, i. 63.
'Opinion, good,' i. 53.
Opposition, described, ii. 29.
Orange, prince of, ii. 97.
Orations, long, of James I., i. 44.
Orbicular, i. 54.
Order, of procedure in House of Commons, ii. 52-3.
Ordinaries, i. 86.
Ought, i. 12.
Overtures, i. 13.
Oxford, adjournment of House of Commons to, i. 123 : plague in, i. 124 ; 'prodigious birth,' i. 126 : speech at, i. 140-8 : parliament at, ii. 8 : driven to, ii. 115.

P.

Palladium, i. 18 : ii. 136.
Pallas, ii. 12.
Pallatinate, i. 51, 57, 76 : ii. 18, 19, 47, 61, 117, 124.
Palsgrave, ii. 47.
Papists, increase of, i. 65, 84 : 'heat' excited by, i. 69 : connivance with, i. 69, 70 : changing names, i. 73 : dangers from, i. 84-5 : no orders to be taken from Rome, i. 89 : employment, i. 164.
Pardons, i. 74 : to a Jesuit, ii. 8, 9, 49.

Parliamentary, if done by parliament, deemed, i. 59.
Parliament of England, i. 33, 34, 35, 36: survey of, i. 37-8: origin of, i. 38: called by Charles I., i. 43: speech of, i. 43: *Parliamentum felix*, i. 48: Charles I. praised for calling, i. 49: derogation of, i. 107: ancient opinions of, i. 130: imperfect, i. 131: privileges of, i. 134: Henry III., recourse to, i. 135-6: advantages of, i. 136: defined, i. 136-7 *et passim*.
Parrie, Sir Thomas, ii. 15.
Particular, and general, i. 29.
'Partie', i. 16, 17.
Passions, i. 29.
Paterculus, i. 104.
Patience, i. 7: sought, i. 7.
Payment of a sum, i. 16.
Peace, 'long corrupted,' i. 41, 42.
Pelion, on Ossa, ii. 128.
Pennie and Gennie (see Binnie), i. 83.
People, the, i. 3, 7, 76.
Performance, not absolute, i. 16.
Perpetuann's, i. 83.
Person, liberty of, ii. 119-123.
Petition, right not grace of, i. 10: petitions, 74, 90, 120: of religion, answered by Buckingham, ii. 57 onward. (See vol. i. 84 onward.)
Petronius, ii. 12.
Phaeton, ii. 36.
Philips, Sir Richard, speech and character, i. 77, 78: ii. 30-1. See *Notes and Illustrations*.

Philistims, i. 71.
Pistle, i. 3.
Plague (see Sickness), i. 123.
Plead, Socrates could not, i. 9.
Pliny, i. 45 ; ii. 121.
Pluralities, i. 87.
Plymouth, ii. 4, *et passim*.
Polipheme, i. 115.
Poll, i. 95.
Pollicie, ii. 144.
Pontoise, loss of, i. 143 ; ii. 87. = Pontoise in France.
Poole, de la, i. 145, 161-2 ; ii. 87, 88, 89 *et passim*.
Poore, i. 90.
Poperie, i. 91, 107.
Popery, ii. 140.
Posterne, i. 97.
Posteritie, i. 6.
Postpos'd, i. 76.
Poundage and tonnage, i. 93.
Poverty and impossibility, i. 157.
Power, absolute, i. 66.
Preaching, to be enlarged, i. 87 ; ridiculed, i. 107.
Precedence, i. 11.
Precedents, i. 9 ; adduced by Sir Edward Coke, ii. 40, 43, 75, 83, 84, 100 ; copies of, ii. 147.
Premeditation, i. 78.
Preparations for war, i. 46, 116 ; ii. 22.
Prerogative, royal, i. 55, 134.
Presage, i. 83.

Presence, access to, i. 53.
Present, i. 46.
President, i. 29, 52.
Prestigious, i. 41, 117 : ii. 6.   See *Notes and Illustrations*.
Pretended, i. 59.
Pretor, i. 35.
Princes, allowance, &c., of, i. 9, 10.
Prioritie, i. 11.
Prisoners of the Fleet, not released in Plague, i. 120.
Prisons, in Papist keeping, i. 88.
Privado's, i. 110, 118.
Privat, publike, i. 11 : right of person, i. 15 : undertaking, i. 70.
Priviledge, i. 8, 9, 11, 13, 14, 15, 17, 21, 23, 26, 28, 60, 102, 134.
Proceedings, with Socrates, i. 7.
Processe, declininge, i. 5, 16, 19.
Proof, not mere words, i. 6.
Prorogation, not adjournment, i. 122.
Protestants, French, ii. 21.
Protest of House of Commons against dissolution, ii. 104 onward : and declaration, ii. 142-7 : against legal proceedings, ii. 147.
Publike, right, i. 9.
Punicke, i. 109.
Punishable, only in Senate, i. 8.
Puritans, i. 107.

Q.

Queen of James, i. 43 : at opening of Parliament, i. 44.
Questor, i. 35.
Quicklime, i. 47.

R.

Reason, i. 7, 36.
Recalling from seminaries, i. 87.
Recess, i. 119.
Recusants, i. 74, 78, 87, 89, 90, 125 : ii. 59.
Reflections, final, ii. 109.
Refractory, i. 20.
Religando, a, i. 71.
Religion, i. 49, 50, 57, 65, 69, 70 : described, i. 70-1 : principle, i. 71 : laws of, i. 72, 74 : and liberty, i. 164 onward : speech of Eliot on, ii. 138-47.
Remedies, ii. 42 onward.
Remonstrance, ii. 116.
Rents, royal, ii. 43.
Reparacon, i. 9.
Resolucon, a judge's, i. 11.
Resources, looked into, ii. 50.
Retention, i. 15, 17.
Retracons, i. 11.
Rhetra, i. 10, 11, 15. See *Notes and Illustrations*.
Rhodians, ii. 135.
Richard II., i. 10, 14, 18, 33.

Rights, i. 5, 10, 13, 14, 22.
Rochellors, ii. 69, 81.
Rome, no order to be taken from, i. 89.
Roper, Lord, ii. 69, 81.
Rubbs, i. 48. See *Notes and Illustrations*.
Rudyard, Sir Benjamin, i. 66: speech of, i. 66-8: not seen the king, i. 68: character of, i. 68-9, 75: petition from, i. 84-5: instruction needed, i. 86: act for, i. 126; five things necessary, ii. 50: petition on, ii. 55.

S.

Sabbath, i. 60, 63, 74, 125.
Sad, i. 12.
Salisburie, earl of, ii. 28.
Samians, i. 149.
Savill, Sir John, i. 61, 95, 96, 97, 100. See *Notes and Illustrations*.
Savoy, duke of, ii. 17 *et passim*.
'Say little but doe much,' i. 55.
Scandall, innocence exposed to, i. 5.
'Sceane,' i. 79: ii. 22.
Schoolmasters, i. 86.
Scotch, i. 35.
Searges, i. 83.
'Seasonable,' commission of greivances not, i. 65.
Sedicon, i. 8.
Seeme, not be, i. 25.
Selden, John, ii. 152.

Seminarie, priests, i. 52, 85, 87.
Senate, publicke, i. 8 : rights of, i. 9, 10, 11, 12, 17, 18, 21, 26, 27.
Seneca, i. 134, 137, 163 : ii. 9, 123.
Sentence, quashed, i. 14.
Session, determination of, i. 120, 126.
Seymour, Sir Francis, speech of, i. 94 : ii. 24, 25. See *Notes and Illustrations.*
Sheriffes, i. 81, 96 : a Yorkshire, i. 103.
Ships, ii. 46.
' Shortlie meet,' i. 119, 123.
Sickness, national, i. 61, 65, 84, 92, 123.
Silence enforct, i. 13, 15.
Sinister intentions, i. 8.
Sociats, i. 27.
Socrates, i. 3 (see also ' Apologie ') : why he defended not himself, i. 3 : dead, memorie of, i. 3, 4 : stained, i. 3 : invoked, i. 4 : silence of, 5 : traitor, i. 5 : worthy to vindicate, i. 6 : power of, if present, i. 6 : memorie of, i. 7 : accusations, i. 7 : not punishable, i. 8 : bound by ' presidents,' i. 9 : the ' stand ' made by, i. 9 : sworn not to reveal debates, i. 13 : point of right, i. 15 : guilty or not, i. 15 : particular charges, i. 16 : expiation of, i. 17 : even if faulty not to be questioned, i. 17, 18, 19 : innocence of, i. 24 : called a traitor, i. 26, 27, 29 : fame of, i. 27 : in person, i. 29 : eulogy, i. 29, 30 : sufferings, i. 30.
Sollicitor, king's, ii. 45. See *Notes and Illustrations.*
Solomon, i. 49, 50.

Somerset, i. 142 : ii. 83.
Spain, i. 35, 41, 42, 56, 143, 168 : ii. 18, 27, 28, 32, 61 *et passim* : match with, ii. 69.
Speaker, choice of, i. 47.
Speech, of Charles I., in opening Parliament, i. 44 : of Lord Keeper (Williams), i. 45-6, 54-9 : free, i. 53 : of Crewe, as Speaker, i. 48-53 : of Philips, ii. 30-6 : of Weston, ii. 36 : of Sir Edward Coke, ii. 39 onward.
Speeches of Sir John Eliot, i. 70-3, 130-9, 139-40, 140-8, 156, 164, 171-80 : ii. 113-18, 119-23, 123-5, 125-30, 130-4.
Spunger, of the commonwealth, i. 136, 161.
Stamford, ii. 120.
Stanneries, ii. 127.
State, i. 8.
Statutes, i. 9.
Strangers, observe felicities of England, i. 33.
Streames, i. 5.
'Subject, one,' ii. 31.
Submission, i. 16.
Submitting, not to authoritie, i. 5.
Subsidies, i. 46, 62, 76, 92, 114, 126, 153-4 : ii. 29, 30, 103. See Gardiner's History, as before, note 1, 288.
Subventions, i. 46.
Sufferance, i. 17.
Suffolk, duke of, i. 144 : ii. 83 (see 'de la Poole').
Supersedeas, i. 15, 73 : ii. 8.
Supplements to *Negotium Posterorum*, i. 127 onward : ii. 111 onward.

'Supply,' i. 75, 76, 110, 117 : ii. 23, 29, 30, 31, 96-7, 98, 113-18, 119-23, 123-5.
Sundaie, unlawful sports, i. 126.
Sweden, king of, ii. 61, 77.
Syneresis, i. 69.

T.

Tacitus, i. 103, 169: ii. 6, 96.
Themistocles, i. 157.
Thrift of Charles I., i. 42.
Tiberius, ii. 96.
Time ('the great commander'), i. 46.
Timotheus, ii. 136.
Tiplings, i. 126.
Titans, ii. 142.
Tobacco, i. 83.
Toledo, ii. 83.
Tongue, of Socrates, i. 6.
Tonnage, i. 93, 109, 125 = so much on the tun of wine and so much on the £ value of other goods.
Townshend, Sir John, i. 80.
Tract, of reason, i. 7.
Tradesmen better than nobles at Admiralty, ii. 44.
Tradition, i. 38.
Traitor, Socrates called, i. 5, 26, 29.
Treaties, dissolution of, i. 42, 48 : no more, ii. 32, 42 ; breach of, ii. 63.
Triall, i. 22.

Troilus, i. 8.
True, even if, not punishable, i. 8.
Trust, the tried, i. 66.
Truth, i. 3, 24.
Turks, 'infestuous,' ii. 3, 4, 5, 93.

U.

'Ulcer canckrous,' i. 132.
Ulysses, i. 115.
'Understanding, no,' i. 130.
Undertakers, i. 132.
Universities, discipline of, i. 86, 87 : livings of, i. 87.
Unparliamentary, i. 46, 59 : ii. 24.
Use, and custome, i. 10.

V.

Valtoline, ii. 27, 61.
Vantgard, ii. 7.
Venetians, i. 83 : ii. 7.
Venice, i. 95.
Verres, i. 159.
Vice, i. 5.
Vindication of Socrates, i. 3, 6.
Virtue, i. 5, 7.

W.

Want, causes of, ii. 42.
War, with Spain, &c., i. 45, 76 : ii. 27, 50.

Wardes, court of, i. 82.
Waste grounds, ii. 43.
Wentworth, Sir Henry (= Strafford), i. 61, 95, 96, 97, 98, 99, 100, 101, 103, 104 : ii. 92.
Weston, Sir Richard, ii. 36, 79. See *Notes and Illustrations, s. n.*
White, Dr., i. 106.
Wickham, Bp., ii. 87, 89. See *Notes and Illustrations.*
Williams, Lord Keeper, i. 45, 92, 140 : ii. 10, 56, 76, 78, 104.
Winter townes = Winterton Ness, i. 81.
Word, virtue gone out of, i. 6.
Writ, i. 20.

Y.

Yorke, presidentship of, and Wales, ii. 41.
Yorkshire, election for, i. 95.
Youth, careful education of, i. 86.—G.

END OF VOL. II.

FINIS.

Uniform with the present volumes.

THE MONARCHIE OF MAN, by Sir John Eliot (1590-1632). Now for the first time printed: from the Author's Manuscript in Harleian Collection (No. 2228). Edited, with Introduction, Notes and Illustrations, Steel Portraits and Facsimiles, &c., by the Rev. Alexander B. Grosart, LL.D., F.S.A., St. George's, Blackburn, Lancashire. In two volumes 4°. 1879. 100 copies only (£2/12/6). Vol. I., pp. 206: Vol. II., pp. 227.

⁎⁎* *Out of print*—and only to be had in a very few sets of the 6 volumes of the Eliot MSS.

In the Press—also uniform.

The great unpublished treatise (in English) on Government and Law, entitled "*De Jure Majestatis*"—from the MSS. at Port Eliot for Earl of St. Germans—with Additions from other unpublished MSS., correspondence, etc. etc. 100 copies only (£2/12/6). In two volumes 4°.

www.ingramcontent.com/pod-product-compliance
Lightning Source LLC
Chambersburg PA
CBHW020907230426
43666CB00008B/1346